# AP
## MACROECONOMICS
### STUDENT WORKBOOK | 5TH EDITION

RUTH COOKSON

MATTHEW GHERMAN

BARBARA BLAKE GONZALEZ

ALEX LAMON

CATHY LATHAM

THEODORE OPDERBECK

STACY QUIROZ-BROWN

**Council for Economic Education**

# AUTHORS

## AUTHORS, FIFTH EDITION

**Matthew Gherman**
*Teacher, Edward R. Murrow High School, New York City, NY*

**Alex Lamon**
*Lead Teacher, Business Education, Livingston High School, Livingston, NJ*

**Cathy Latham**
*Retired Educator*

**Theodore Opderbeck**
*Social Studies Teacher, Waldwick High School, Waldwick, NJ*

**Stacy Quiroz-Brown**
*Economic Education Teacher Advisor, Arizona Council on Economic Education*


## AUTHORS, FOURTH EDITION

**Margaret A. Ray**

**Gary L. Stone**


## PROJECT DIRECTOR/AUTHOR

**Ruth Cookson**
*Senior Manager, Educational Content*
*Council for Economic Education*


## EDITOR/AUTHOR

**Barbara Blake Gonzalez**
*Chief Administrative Officer, The Dragas Center for Economic Analysis and Policy,*
*Department of Economics, Strome College of Business, Old Dominion University*


## DIGITAL CONSULTANT/PROJECT MANAGER

**Veronica Tomaiuolo**

**This publication was made possible through funding by the WoodNext Foundation.**

ISBN: 978-1-7348096-4-0

# TABLE OF CONTENTS

# TABLE OF CONTENTS

# UNIT 1
## BASIC ECONOMIC CONCEPTS

# UNIT 1 **MACROECONOMICS KEY IDEAS**

- Scarcity exists because we have limited resources and unlimited wants. No society has ever had enough resources to produce all the goods and services its members wanted.

- Goods and services are produced from resources. These resources—land, labor, capital, and entrepreneurship—are limited.

- Scarcity requires people to make choices. If we use scarce resources for one purpose, we cannot use them for another.

- Opportunity cost is the forgone benefit of the next best alternative when resources are used for one purpose rather than another.

- Because of scarcity, every decision has an opportunity cost.

- Economic costs take account of the opportunity cost of doing one thing rather than another.

- Economic costs include explicit costs and implicit costs. Explicit costs are expenditures for something. Implicit costs are the opportunity costs of using your own resources rather than selling them to someone else. Both implicit and explicit costs are opportunity costs.

- Using free goods does not involve opportunity cost because free goods are available in unlimited quantities.

- Economics is concerned with marginal decision making. In economics, "making decisions at the margin" is very important. Marginal choices involve the effects of additions and subtractions from the current situation. We compare the marginal benefit of an extra unit of an activity with that unit's marginal cost.

- A production possibilities curve can be used to illustrate scarcity, choice, and opportunity cost graphically.

- The slope of a production possibilities curve shows the opportunity cost of producing another unit of one good in terms of the amount of the other good that must be given up.

- Because resources are scarce, using them efficiently allows us to get the most from them. Efficiency is increased through specialization and trade.

- Economists use the concept of comparative advantage to explain why trade takes place between countries and between individuals. This concept is based on the differences in producers' opportunity costs of producing goods and services.

- Absolute advantage describes a situation in which an individual, business, or country can produce more of a good or service than any other producer with the same quantity of resources.

- Comparative advantage describes a situation in which an individual, business, or country can produce a good or service at a lower opportunity cost than another producer.

- Production specialization according to comparative advantage results in exchange opportunities that lead to consumption opportunities beyond the PPC.

- The test of an economic theory is its ability to correctly predict the future consequences of economic actions.

- The broad social goals of a society influence decisions about how best to use resources.

- Markets bring together buyers and sellers of a good or service.

- The law of demand states that buyers will want more of an item at a low price than at a high price, other things being equal.

- The law of supply states that sellers will provide more of an item at a high price than at a low price, other things being equal.

- The equilibrium price is the price at which the quantity demanded of an item equals the quantity supplied. That quantity is called the equilibrium quantity.

- Shifts in the market demand and supply curves result in new values of the equilibrium price and quantity.

- Market prices that are higher than the equilibrium price result in surpluses; market prices that are lower than the equilibrium price result in shortages. Whenever markets experience imbalances—creating disequilibrium prices, surpluses, and shortages—market forces drive prices toward equilibrium.

# Do You Think Like an Economist?

**Circle T for true or F for false in the statements that follow.**

T  F  1.  Because it is desirable, sunshine is scarce.

T  F  2.  Because it is limited, polio is scarce.

T  F  3.  Because water covers three-fourths of the earth's surface and is renewable, it cannot be considered scarce.

T  F  4.  The main cost of going to college is tuition, room, and board.

T  F  5.  If electric companies raise their rates, consumers will use the same amount of electricity anyway.

T  F  6.  You get what you pay for.

T  F  7.  If someone makes an economic gain, someone else loses.

T  F  8.  If one nation produces everything better than another nation, there is no economic reason for these two nations to trade.

T  F  9.  I'm quitting my job and taking one that has better pay. There are no secondary effects from this action.

T  F  10.  A business owner's decision to show more care for consumers is a decision to accept lower levels of profits.

# UNIT 1 ACTIVITY 1-2.1

# Scarcity and Opportunity Costs

## Directions: For each of the following questions, Identify the implicit cost or explicit cost.

1. At lunch, Devin has the choice of a hamburger, pizza, or salad. He really wants the pizza but decides to eat healthier and chooses the salad.

2. Diego owns an ice cream shop in a local tourist town. Last month he earned $5,000 in profits. He chose to use the $5,000 to purchase a new freezer.

3. Kay is a very talented swimmer. On some days she really wants to skip practice and spend time with her friends. When this happens, she thinks about her goal of swimming in the State Finals so she goes to practice.

4. Nafez owns a company that produces paper clips and staples. Due to increased demand for paper clips he decides to convert part of his staple assembly line to paper clips.

5. David has a job earning $15 per hour. He decides to take four hours off of work to go hiking with his friends.

6. Valeria has a big test in economics tomorrow. She is trying to decide if she should study another 10 minutes or quit studying to watch her favorite television show. She decides to study another 10 minutes.

7. A local government is completing its budget. It needs money for school improvements, road improvements and the fire department. It had planned on spending the money on school improvements and the fire department, but after meeting with taxpayers, it decided to put the money toward road improvements.

# Scarcity, Opportunity Cost, and Production Possibilities Curves

The opportunity cost of using scarce resources for one thing instead of something else is often represented in graphical form as a *production possibilities curve* (PPC). A nation's PPC shows how many units of two goods or services the nation can produce in one year if it uses its resources fully and efficiently. This activity uses the PPC to illustrate how scarcity requires choices and the opportunity cost of those choices.

## Part A: Basic Production Possibilities Curves

Figure 1-3.1 shows a basic PPC for the production of Goods A and B. Use Figure 1-3.1 to answer the questions that follow.

*Figure 1-3.1*
**A LINEAR PRODUCTION POSSIBILITIES CURVE**

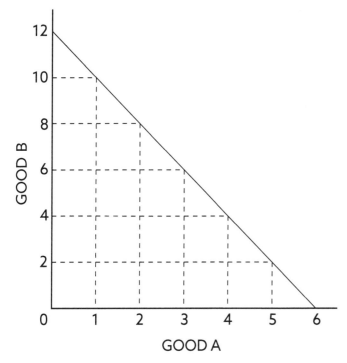

1. Assume the economy represented by Figure 1-3.1 is presently producing 12 units of Good B and 0 units of Good A:

   • The opportunity cost of increasing production of Good A from 0 units to 1 unit is the loss of ____ unit(s) of Good B.

   • The opportunity cost of increasing production of Good A from 1 unit to 2 units is the loss of ____ unit(s) of Good B.

   • The opportunity cost of increasing production of Good A from 2 units to 3 units is the loss of ____ unit(s) of Good B.

   • This is an example of *(constant/increasing/decreasing/zero)* opportunity cost per unit for Good A.

Figure 1-3.2 contains a typical PPC often used by economists. This PPC is concave to the origin; it gets steeper as the country moves out along its horizontal axis. Use Figure 1-3.2 to answer the questions below it.

*Figure 1-3.2*
## A CONCAVE PRODUCTION POSSIBILITIES CURVE

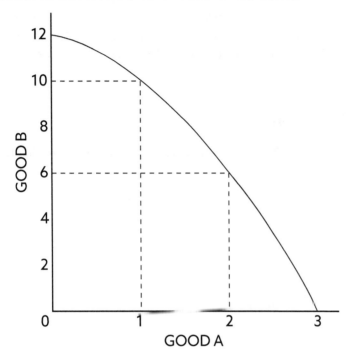

2. If the economy represented in Figure 1-3.2 is presently producing 12 units of Good B and 0 units of Good A:

   • The opportunity cost of increasing production of Good A from 0 units to 1 unit is the loss of ____ unit(s) of Good B.

   • The opportunity cost of increasing production of Good A from 1 unit to 2 units is the loss of ____ unit(s) of Good B.

   • The opportunity cost of increasing production of Good A from 2 units to 3 units is the loss of ____ unit(s) of Good B.

   • This is an example of (*constant/increasing/decreasing/zero*) opportunity cost per unit for Good A.

## Part B: Understanding the Shape of a Concave PPC

*Figure 1-3.3*
**THE LAW OF INCREASING OPPORTUNITY COST**

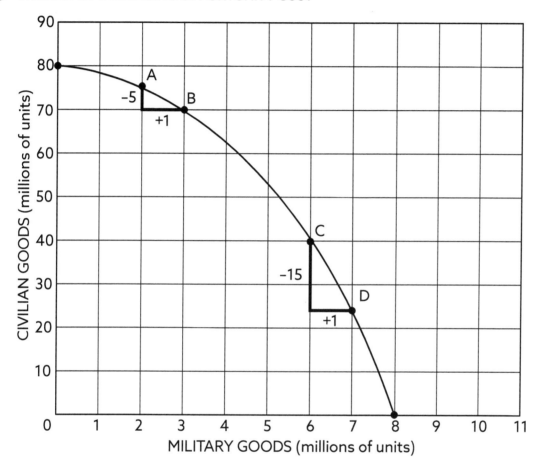

The "law of increasing opportunity cost" explains why the typical PPC is concave to the origin (bowed outward). Figure 1-3.3 shows the PPC for the country of Costica.

1. The country of Costica currently operates at point A and produces 75 million units of civilian goods and 2 million units of military goods. If the country decides to increase its military provision to 3 million units, it must give up only _____ million units in civilian goods because certain factors of production are easily converted from civilian production to military production.

2. However, if Costica decides it must continue to increase its military production, the opportunity cost of doing so (increases/decreases). Why?

3. The opportunity cost of increasing military output from 6 million units to 7 million units (point C to point D) has increased to _____ million units in civilian goods. This increasing opportunity cost is reflected in the steeper slope of the PPC as the country produces (more/fewer) military goods and (more/fewer) civilian goods.

## Part C: Drawing Various PPCs

Use the following axes to draw the type of curve that illustrates the label above each graph.

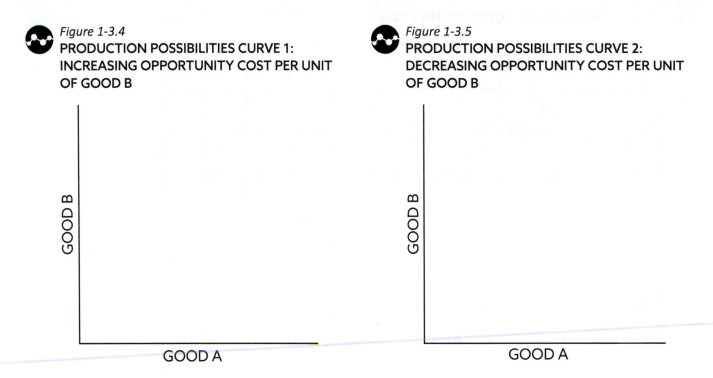

*Figure 1-3.4*
**PRODUCTION POSSIBILITIES CURVE 1: INCREASING OPPORTUNITY COST PER UNIT OF GOOD B**

*Figure 1-3.5*
**PRODUCTION POSSIBILITIES CURVE 2: DECREASING OPPORTUNITY COST PER UNIT OF GOOD B**

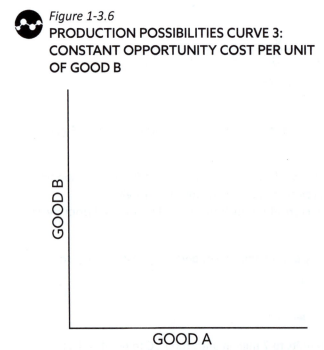

*Figure 1-3.6*
**PRODUCTION POSSIBILITIES CURVE 3: CONSTANT OPPORTUNITY COST PER UNIT OF GOOD B**

# UNIT 1 **ACTIVITY 1-3.1** (continued)

## Part D: Economic Growth

Over time, most countries see an increase in their ability to produce goods and services. This "economic growth" is shown as an outward shift of the PPC and results from a variety of factors, including improved technology, better education, and the discovery of new resources. Use Figure 1-3.7 to answer the next six questions. Each question starts with Curve BE as a country's PPC.

*Figure 1-3.7*
**PRODUCTION POSSIBILITIES CURVE: CAPITAL GOODS AND CONSUMER GOODS**

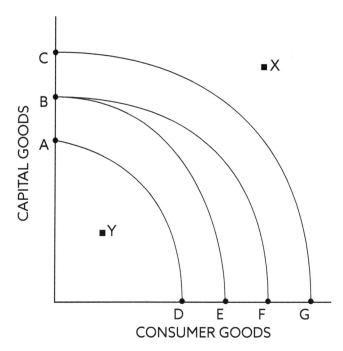

Each question starts with Curve BE as a country's PPC.

1.  Suppose there is a major technological breakthrough in only the consumer-goods industry, and the new technology is widely adopted. Which curve in the diagram would represent the new PPC? (Indicate the curve you choose with two letters.) _____

2.  Suppose there are major technological innovations in both industries. Which curve in the diagram would represent the new PPC? (Indicate the curve you choose with two letters.) _____

3.  Suppose a new government comes into power and forbids the use of automated machinery and modern production techniques in all industries. Which curve in the diagram would represent the new PPC? (Indicate the curve you choose with two letters.) _____

4.  Suppose massive new sources of oil and coal are found within the economy. Which curve in the diagram would represent the new PPC? (Indicate the curve you choose with two letters.) _____

5.  If BE represents a country's current PPC, what can you say about a point like X? (Write a brief statement.)



6.  If BE represents a country's current PPC, what can you say about a point like Y? (Write a brief statement.)

Use Figure 1-3.8 to answer the next three questions.

*Figure 1-3.8*
**PRODUCTION POSSIBILITIES CURVE: ECONOMIC GROWTH**

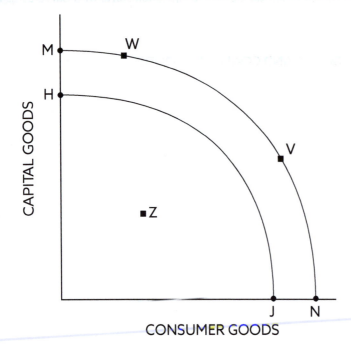

7.  What change could cause the PPC to shift from the original curve (HJ) to the new curve (MN)?

8.  Under what conditions might an economy be operating at Point Z?

9.  Why might a government implement a policy to encourage the economy to move from Point V to Point W? Student Reminder: A consumer good is intended for final use by individuals; a capital good is used to produce other goods and services.

# Determining Comparative Advantage

Voluntary trade between two individuals or two countries occurs if both parties feel that they will benefit. Producers have an incentive to make products for which they have a lower opportunity cost than other producers. When both producers specialize according to their comparative advantage, they increase the total amount of goods and services that are available for consumption. To determine who has a comparative advantage in producing a particular item, we need to calculate each producer's opportunity costs of creating the items. The way we calculate opportunity cost depends on how the productivity data is expressed.

There are two ways to measure productivity: the "input method" and the "output method." We can calculate the quantity of output produced from a given amount of inputs, or we can measure the amount of inputs necessary to create one unit of output. Examples of output are bushels of wheat per acre, miles per gallon, words per minute, apples per tree, and televisions produced per hour. Examples of input are the number of hours to do a job, number of gallons of paint to paint a house, and number of acres to feed a horse.

## Part A: Two Approaches to Comparative Advantage

> Student Alert: In using these models to determine the lower opportunity costs from both an input and output viewpoint, you must pay attention to the format of the chart. It makes a difference! ⊙

## Input Method

The "input method" provides data on the amount of resources needed to produce one unit of output. Table 1-4.1 gives productivity information for Hakeem and Sita.

*Table 1-4.1*
**PRODUCTIVITY DATA USING THE INPUT METHOD**

|  | Time required to produce one radio | Time required to produce one bushel of wheat |
|---|---|---|
| Hakeem | 20 minutes | 5 minutes |
| Sita | 30 minutes | 15 minutes |

Hakeem has an absolute advantage in the production of both radios and wheat because he uses fewer resources (time) to produce each item than does Sita. Even though this might suggest that Hakeem cannot benefit from trade with Sita, our examination of the opportunity costs of production will show that is not the case.

*Table 1-4.2*
**OPPORTUNITY COST OF PRODUCING RADIOS AND WHEAT**

|  | Opportunity cost of producing one radio | Opportunity cost of producing one bushel of wheat |
|---|---|---|
| Hakeem | 1 radio $= \dfrac{20 \text{ minutes}}{5 \text{ minutes}} = 4$ bushels | 1 wheat $= \dfrac{5 \text{ minutes}}{20 \text{ minutes}} = ¼$ radio |
| Sita | 1 radio $= \dfrac{30 \text{ minutes}}{15 \text{ minutes}} = 2$ bushels | 1 wheat $= \dfrac{15 \text{ minutes}}{30 \text{ minutes}} = ½$ radio |

In the 20 minutes it takes Hakeem to produce one radio, he instead could have produced four bushels of wheat. Instead of producing one radio in 30 minutes, Sita could have produced two bushels of wheat. The fact that Sita has the lower opportunity cost of producing radios means she has the comparative advantage in radios.

In the five minutes he needs to produce one bushel of wheat, Hakeem could have made ¼ of a radio. Sita's opportunity cost of producing one bushel of wheat is ½ of a radio. Because his sacrifice in producing one bushel of wheat is less than Sita's, Hakeem has the comparative advantage in wheat production.

If Hakeem specializes in wheat production while Sita specializes in radio production, their combined output of radios and wheat will be larger than it would be if each person produced both products.

## Output Method

The "output method" gives data on the amount of output that can be produced with a given amount of an input. Now let's take this same set of productivity data and turn it into an output format. To do this, we ask how many units of an item the producers can create with a given amount of resources. Let's suppose that both producers have one hour to produce each product. Table 1-4.3 shows how many radios and how many bushels of wheat each producer can make in one hour. From this output viewpoint, you once again see that Hakeem has the absolute advantage in the production of both products. With the same amount of resources (one hour of labor), he can produce more radios and more wheat than Sita.

*Table 1-4.3*
**PRODUCTIVITY DATA USING THE OUTPUT METHOD**

|  | Radios produced per hour | Wheat produced per hour |
|---|---|---|
| Hakeem | $\dfrac{60 \text{ minutes}}{20 \text{ minutes}} = 3$ radios | $\dfrac{60 \text{ minutes}}{5 \text{ minutes}} = 12$ bushels |
| Sita | $\dfrac{60 \text{ minutes}}{30 \text{ minutes}} = 2$ radios | $\dfrac{60 \text{ minutes}}{15 \text{ minutes}} = 4$ bushels |

But what about the opportunity cost to produce each item? Check out Table 1-4.4, which shows how to calculate each producer's opportunity cost of the two items. To find Hakeem's opportunity cost of producing one radio, the number of radios he can produce in one hour goes under the number of bushels of wheat he can produce in that same time frame.

*Table 1-4.4*
### OPPORTUNITY COST OF PRODUCING RADIOS AND WHEAT

| | Opportunity cost of producing one radio | Opportunity cost of producing one bushel of wheat |
|---|---|---|
| Hakeem | 3 radios = 1 hour = 12 bushels<br>1 radio = 12/3 = 4 bushels | 12 bushels = 1 hour = 3 radios<br>1 bushel = 3/12 = ¼ radio |
| Sita | 2 radios = 1 hour = 4 bushels<br>1 radio = 4/2 = 2 bushels | 4 bushels = 1 hour = 2 radios<br>1 bushel = 2/4 = ½ radio |

Because Hakeem's cost per radio is four bushels of wheat, whereas Sita's cost per radio is only two bushels, we know Sita has the comparative advantage in producing radios. Hakeem has the comparative advantage in wheat production since he has the lower opportunity cost of producing a bushel of wheat (¼ radio compared to Sita's ½ radio). Does this sound familiar? This is the same result we reached using the input method.

The differences in opportunity costs define the limits of a trade in which both parties will benefit. If Sita specializes in radio production, she will accept no less than two bushels of wheat for one radio. Hakeem will pay no more than four bushels of wheat per radio. Thus, the "terms of trade" acceptable to both producers must lie in the range between two bushels for one radio and four bushels for one radio. For example, suppose they agree to trade one radio for three bushels of wheat. By producing and trading one radio to Hakeem, Sita will have a net gain of one bushel. Her opportunity cost of producing the radio is two bushels and she receives three bushels in return for the radio. Because his opportunity cost of producing one bushel is ¼ radio, Hakeem's opportunity cost of producing the three bushels, which he trades to Sita, is ¾ radio. Thus, the trade gives Hakeem a net gain of ¼ radio. Both producers gain by specializing according to their comparative advantage.

When it comes to producing wheat, Hakeem would have to receive at least ¼ of a radio in trade for a bushel of wheat. Sita would require at least ½ of a radio before she would trade a bushel of wheat. The acceptable terms of trade would be found between ¼ radio and ½ radio per bushel of wheat. By specializing and trading, both Hakeem and Sita can consume (not produce) outside of their production possibility curve.

The output data in Table 1-4.3 can be used to create production possibility frontiers for Hakeem and Sita to show the combinations of radios and wheat each can produce in one hour of work. See Figure 1-4.1.

*Figure 1-4.1*
**PRODUCTION POSSIBILITIES CURVES FOR HAKEEM AND SITA**

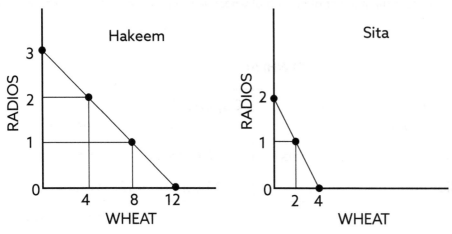

## Part B: Comparative Advantage Exercises

For each of the following scenarios, answer the questions following the chart.

Kiara and Barry can grow the following amounts of potatoes and cabbage with a week of labor.

|        | Potatoes per week | Cabbage per week |
|--------|-------------------|------------------|
| Kiara  | 100 units         | 200 units        |
| Barry  | 120 units         | 150 units        |

1. Is this an example of an input problem or an output problem?

2.  What is the opportunity cost for each producer in making these products? Show your work.

    (A)  Kiara's opportunity cost of producing a unit of potatoes is _____ units of cabbage.

    (B)  Barry's opportunity cost of producing a unit of potatoes is _____ units of cabbage.

    (C)  Kiara's opportunity cost of producing a unit of cabbage is _____ units of potatoes.

    (D)  Barry's opportunity cost of producing a unit of cabbage is _____ units of potatoes.

3.  Who has the comparative advantage in producing potatoes? _____

4.  Who has the comparative advantage in producing cabbage? _____

    *Note:* In this example, each producer has the absolute advantage in producing one item: Barry in potatoes and Kiara in cabbage. That might not be the case in the other examples.

Elijah and Jocelyn fish for bass and catfish. This chart shows how many of each type of fish they can catch in one day.

|  | Bass | Catfish |
| --- | --- | --- |
| Elijah | 4 bass | 6 catfish |
| Jocelyn | 24 bass | 12 catfish |

5.  Is this an example of an input problem or an output problem?

6.  What is the opportunity cost for each person in catching these fish?

    (A)  Elijah's opportunity cost of catching 1 bass is _____ catfish.

    (B)  Jocelyn's opportunity cost of catching 1 bass is _____ catfish.

    (C)  Elijah's opportunity cost of catching 1 catfish is _____ bass.

    (D)  Jocelyn's opportunity cost of catching 1 catfish is _____ bass.

7. Who has the comparative advantage in catching bass? _____

8. Who has the comparative advantage in catching catfish? _____

9. This chart shows how many days it takes the ABC Corporation and the XYZ Corporation to produce one unit of cars and one unit of planes.

|  | Cars | Planes |
|---|---|---|
| ABC Corp. | 8 days | 10 days |
| XYZ Corp. | 15 days | 12 days |

10. Is this an example of an input problem or an output problem?

11. What is the opportunity cost for each corporation in producing these goods?

    (A) ABC's opportunity cost of producing a unit of cars is _____ units of planes.

    (B) XYZ's opportunity cost of producing a unit of cars is _____ units of planes.

    (C) ABC's opportunity cost of producing a unit of planes is _____ units of cars.

    (D) XYZ's opportunity cost of producing a unit of planes is _____ units of cars.

12. Who has the comparative advantage in producing cars? _____

13. Who has the comparative advantage in producing planes? _____

Here are the numbers of acres needed in India and China to produce 100 bushels of corn or 100 bushels of rice each month.

|  | India | China |
|---|---|---|
| Corn | 9 acres | 8 acres |
| Rice | 3 acres | 2 acres |

14. Is this an example of an input problem or an output problem?

15. What is the opportunity cost for each country in producing these goods?

   (A) India's opportunity cost of growing 100 bushels of corn is _____ bushels of rice.

   (B) China's opportunity cost of growing 100 bushels of corn is _____ bushels of rice.

   (C) India's opportunity cost of growing 100 bushels of rice is _____ bushels of corn.

   (D) opportunity cost of growing 100 bushels of rice is _____ bushels of corn.

16. Who has the comparative advantage in growing corn? _____

17. Who has the comparative advantage in growing rice? _____

This chart shows how many cans of olives and bottles of olive oil can be produced in Zaire and Colombia from one ton of olives.

|  | Zaire | Colombia |
|---|---|---|
| Olives | 60 cans | 24 cans |
| Olive oil | 10 bottles | 8 bottles |

18. Is this an example of an input problem or an output problem?

19. What is the opportunity cost for each country in producing these goods?

   (A) Zaire's opportunity cost of producing 1 can of olives is _____ bottles of olive oil.

   (B) Colombia's opportunity cost of producing 1 can of olives is _____ bottles of olive oil.

   (C) Zaire's opportunity cost of producing 1 bottle of olive oil is _____ cans of olives.

   (D) Colombia's opportunity cost of producing 1 bottle of olive oil is _____ cans of olives.

20. Who has the comparative advantage in producing olives? _____

21. Who has the comparative advantage in producing olive oil? _____

# Demand Curves, Movements Along Demand Curves, and Shifts in Demand Curves

## Part A: A Change in Demand versus a Change in Quantity Demanded

Student Alert: The distinction between a "change in demand" and a "change in quantity demanded" is very important!

Table 1-5.1 shows the market demand for Gumballs. Study the data and plot the demand for Gumballs on the graph in Figure 1-5.1. Label the demand curve D, and answer the questions that follow.

*Table 1-5.1*
**DEMAND FOR GUMBALLS**

| Price (per Gumball) | Quantity demanded per week (millions of Gumballs) |
|---|---|
| $0.10 | 350 |
| $0.15 | 300 |
| $0.20 | 250 |
| $0.25 | 200 |
| $0.30 | 150 |
| $0.35 | 100 |
| $0.40 | 50 |
| $0.45 | 0 |

*Figure 1-5.1*
**DEMAND FOR GUMBALLS**

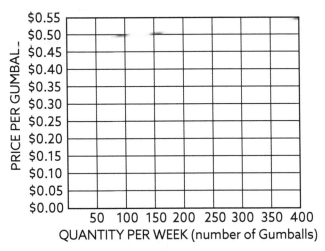

1. The data for demand curve D indicate that at a price of $0.30 per gumball, buyers would be willing to buy _____ Gumballs. All other things held constant, if the price of Gumballs increased to $0.40 per gumball, buyers would be willing to buy _____ Gumballs. Such a change would be a decrease in (demand/quantity demanded). All other things held constant, if the price of Gumballs decreased to $0.20, buyers would be willing to buy _____ Gumballs. Such a change would be called an increase in (demand/quantity demanded).

Now, let's suppose there is a change in federal income-tax rates that affects the disposable income of gumball buyers. This change in the *ceteris paribus* (all else being equal) conditions underlying the original demand for Gumballs will result in a new set of data, shown in Table 1-5.2. Study these new data, and add the new demand curve for Gumballs to the graph in Figure 1-5.1 Label the new demand curve $D_1$ and answer the questions that follow.

*Table 1-5.2*
**NEW DEMAND FOR GUMBALLS**

| Price (per Gumball) | Quantity demanded per week (number of Gumballs) |
|---|---|
| $0.05 | 300 |
| $0.10 | 250 |
| $0.15 | 200 |
| $0.20 | 150 |
| $0.25 | 100 |
| $0.30 | 50 |

2. Comparing the new demand curve ($D_1$) with the original demand curve (D), we can say that the change in the demand for Gumballs results in a shift of the demand curve to the (left/right). Such a shift indicates that at each of the possible prices shown, buyers are now willing to buy a (smaller/larger) quantity; and at each of the possible quantities shown, buyers are willing to offer a (higher/lower) maximum price. The cause of this demand curve shift was a(n) (increase/ decrease) in tax rates that (increased/decreased) the disposable income of gumball buyers.

Now, let's suppose that there is a dramatic change in people's tastes and preferences for Gumballs. This change in the ceteris paribus conditions underlying the original demand for Gumballs will result in a new set of data, shown in Table 1-5.3. Study these new data, and add the new demand curve for Gumballs to the graph in Figure 1-5.1. Label the new demand curve $D_2$ and answer the questions that follow.

*Table 1-5.3*
**NEW DEMAND FOR GUMBALLS**

| Price (per Gumball) | Quantity demanded per week (number of Gumballs) |
|---|---|
| $0.20 | 350 |
| $0.25 | 300 |
| $0.30 | 250 |
| $0.35 | 200 |
| $0.40 | 150 |
| $0.45 | 100 |
| $0.50 | 50 |

3. Comparing this new demand curve (D2) with the original demand curve (D), we can say that the change in the demand for Gumballs results in a shift of the demand curve to the (left/right). Such a shift indicates that at each of the possible prices shown, buyers are now willing to buy a (smaller/larger) quantity; and at each of the possible quantities shown, buyers are willing to offer a (lower/higher) maximum price. The cause of this shift in the demand curve was a(n) (increase/decrease) in people's tastes and preferences for Gumballs.

## Part B: Do You Get It?

Now, to test your understanding, choose the answer you think is the best in each of the following multiple-choice questions.

4.  All other things held constant, which of the following would not cause a change in the demand (shift in the demand curve) for motorcycles?

    (A)  A decrease in consumer incomes

    (B)  A decrease in the price of motorcycles. This will cause an increase in the "quantity demanded" of motorcycles.

    (C)  An increase in the price of bicycles

    (D)  An increase in the price of bicycle helmets

    (E)  An increase in people's tastes and preferences for motorcycles

5.  "Rising oil prices have caused a sharp decrease in the demand for oil." Speaking precisely, and using terms as they are defined by economists, choose the statement that best describes this quotation.

    (A)  The quotation is correct: an increase in price causes a decrease in demand.

    (B)  The quotation is incorrect: an increase in price causes an increase in demand, not a decrease in demand.

    (C)  The quotation is incorrect: an increase in price causes a decrease in the quantity demanded, not a decrease in demand.

    (D)  The quotation is incorrect: an increase in price causes an increase in the quantity demanded, not a decrease in demand.

    (E)  The quotation is correct: the sharp decrease in demand for oil has caused the rise in prices.

6.  "As the price of domestic automobiles has risen, customers have found foreign autos to be a better bargain. Consequently, domestic auto sales have been decreasing, and foreign auto sales have been increasing." Using only the information in this quotation and assuming everything else remains constant, which of the following best describes this statement?

    (A)  A shift in the demand curves for both domestic and foreign automobiles

    (B)  A movement along the demand curves for both foreign and domestic automobiles

    (C)  A movement along the demand curve for domestic autos, and a shift in the demand curve for foreign autos

    (D)  A shift in the demand curve for domestic autos, and a movement along the demand curve for foreign autos

    (E)  A shift in the demand curve for domestic autos, and no movement along the demand curve for foreign autos.

## Part C: Consumer Surplus

Once we have the demand curve, we can define the concept of *consumer surplus*. Consumer surplus is the value a consumer receives from the purchase of a good in excess of the price paid for the good. Stated differently, consumer surplus is the difference between the amount a person is willing and able to pay for a unit of the good and the actual price paid for that unit. For example, if you are willing to pay $100 for a coat but are able to buy the coat for only $70, you have a consumer surplus of $30.

Refer again to the demand data from Table 1-5.1, and assume the price is $0.30. Some buyers will benefit because they are willing to pay prices higher than $0.30 for this good. Note that each time the price is reduced by $0.05, consumers will buy an additional 50 Gumballs. Table 1-5.4 shows how to calculate the consumer surplus resulting from the price of $0.30.

*Table 1-5.4*
**FINDING THE CONSUMER SURPLUS WHEN THE PRICE IS $0.30**

| Price willing to pay | Quantity demanded | Consumer surplus from the increments of 50 units if P = $0.30 |
|---|---|---|
| $0.40 | 50 units | ($0.10)(50 units) = $5.00 |
| $0.35 | 100 units | ($0.05)(50 units) = $2.50 |
| $0.30 | 150 units | ($0.00)(50 units) = $0.00 |

The Price for each unit is $0.30. For those consumers willing to buy 50 units at a price of $0.40, the consumer surplus for each unit is $0.10 (= $0.40 the highest price that consumers are willing to pay minus the current price of $0.30 or $0.40 – $0.30), making the consumer surplus for all these units equal to $5.00.

If the price is reduced from $0.40 to $0.35, consumers who paid $0.40 are also willing to buy at $0.35 and buy another 50 units; the consumer surplus for these buyers is $0.05 per unit ($0.35 – $0.30) or a total of $2.50 for those 50 units.

If the price is lowered another $0.05 to $0.30, an extra 50 units will be demanded; the consumer surplus for these units is $0.00 since $0.30 is the highest price these consumers are willing to pay.

Thus, if the price is $0.30, a total of 150 units are demanded and the total consumer surplus is $7.50.

## Part D: Calculating Consumer Surplus Using a Graph

An approximation of the total consumer surplus from a given number of units of a good can be shown graphically as the area below the demand curve and above the price paid for those units. In Figure 1-5.2, redraw the demand curve (D) from the data in Table 1-5.1. We see that if the price is $0.30, the quantity demanded is 150 units. Consumer surplus from these 150 units is the shaded area between the demand curve D and the horizontal price line at $0.30. We can find the area of this triangle using the familiar rule of (½) × base × height.

*Figure 1-5.2*
CONSUMER SURPLUS

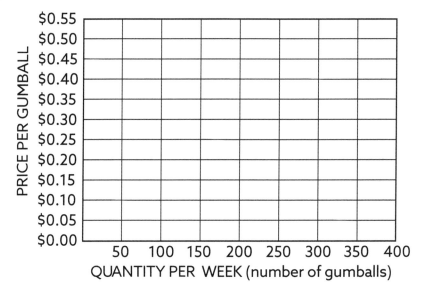

7. What is the value of consumer surplus in this market if the price is $0.30? _____ Write the equation showing how you calculated the value of the area of the triangle representing consumer surplus.

8. Answer these questions based on the discussion of Figure 1-5.2.

   (A) If the price is increased from $0.30 to $0.35, consumer surplus will (increase/decrease). Why?

   (B) If the price is decreased from $0.30 to $0.25, consumer surplus will (increase/decrease). Why?

# Reasons for Changes in Demand

## Part A: Does the Demand Curve Shift?

Read the eight newspaper headlines in Table 1-5.5, and use the table to record the impact of each event on the demand for U.S.-made autos. In the second column, indicate whether the event in the headline will cause consumers to buy more or less U.S.-made autos. Use the third column to indicate whether there is a change in demand (ΔD) or a change in quantity demanded (ΔQd) for U.S.-made autos. In the fourth column, decide whether the demand curve shifts to the right or left or does not shift. Finally, in the last column draw and label the graph showing the shift in the curve for U.S.-made autos.

*Table 1-5.5*
**IMPACT OF EVENTS ON DEMAND FOR U.S.-MADE AUTOS**

| Headline | Will consumers buy more or less U.S. autos? | Is there a change in demand (ΔD) or a change in quantity demanded (ΔQd)? | Does the demand curve for U.S. autos shift to the right or left or not shift? | Draw and label the graph showing the shift in the curve for U.S. autos. |
|---|---|---|---|---|
| 1. Consumers' Income Drops | More / Less | ΔD / ΔQd | Right / Left / No Shift | |
| 2. Millions of Immigrants Enter the U.S. | More / Less | ΔD / ΔQd | Right / Left / No Shift | |
| 3. Price of Foreign Autos Drop | More / Less | ΔD / ΔQd | Right / Left / No Shift | |
| 4. Major Cities Add Inexpensive Bus Lines | More / Less | ΔD / ΔQd | Right / Left / No Shift | |
| 5. Price of U.S. Autos Rises | More / Less | ΔD / ΔQd | Right / Left / No Shift | |
| 6. Price of U.S. Autos Expected to Rise Soon | More / Less | ΔD / ΔQd | Right / Left / No Shift | |
| 7. Families Look Forward to Summer Vacations | More / Less | ΔD / ΔQd | Right / Left / No Shift | |
| 8. U.S. Auto Firms Launch Effective Ad Campaigns | More / Less | ΔD / ΔQd | Right / Left / No Shift | |

## Part B: Why Does the Demand Curve Shift?

Categorize each change in demand in Part A according to the reason why demand changed. A given demand curve assumes that consumer expectations, consumer tastes, the number of consumers in the market, the income of consumers, and the prices of substitutes and complements are unchanged. In Table 1-5.6, place an X next to the reason that the event described in the headline caused a change in demand. One headline will have no answer because it will result in a change in quantity demanded rather than a change in demand.

*Table 1-5.6*
**REASONS FOR A CHANGE IN DEMAND FOR U.S.-MADE AUTOS**

| Reason | Headline number | | | | | | | |
|---|---|---|---|---|---|---|---|---|
| | 1 | 2 | 3 | 4 | 5 | 6 | 7 | 8 |
| 9. A change in consumer expectations | | | | | | | | |
| 10. A change in consumer taste | | | | | | | | |
| 11. A change in the number of consumer in the market | | | | | | | | |
| 12. A change in income | | | | | | | | |
| 13. A change in the price of a substitute good | | | | | | | | |
| 14. A change in the price of a complementary good | | | | | | | | |

# Supply Curves, Movements along Supply Curves, and Shifts in Supply Curves

In this activity, we will assume that the supply curve of Gumballs is upward sloping.

## Part A: A Change in Supply versus a Change in Quantity Supplied

> Student Alert: The distinction between a "change in supply" and a "change in quantity supplied" is very important!

Study the data in Table 1-6.1 and plot the supply of Gumballs on the graph in Figure 1-6.1. Label the supply curve S and answer the questions that follow.

*Table 1-6.1*
**SUPPLY OF GUMBALLS**

| Price (per Gumball) | Quantity supplied per week (number of Gumballs) |
|---|---|
| $0.05 | 0 |
| $0.10 | 50 |
| $0.15 | 100 |
| $0.20 | 150 |
| $0.25 | 200 |
| $0.30 | 250 |
| $0.35 | 300 |
| $0.40 | 350 |

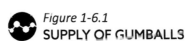

*Figure 1-6.1*
**SUPPLY OF GUMBALLS**

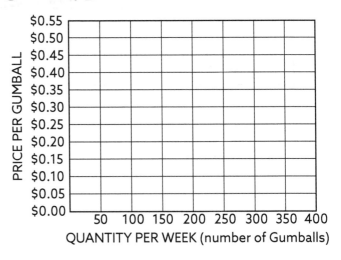

1. The data for supply curve S indicate that at a price of $0.25 per gumball, suppliers would be willing to offer _____ Gumballs. All other things held constant, if the price of Gumballs increased to $0.30 per Gumball, suppliers would be willing to offer _____ Gumballs. Such a change would be an increase in (supply/quantity supplied). All other things held constant, if the price of Gumballs decreased to $0.20 per Gumball, suppliers would be willing to offer _____ Gumballs. Such a change would be called a decrease in (supply/quantity supplied).

Now, let's suppose that there is a change in the price of several of the raw materials used in making Gumballs. This change in the ceteris paribus conditions underlying the original supply of Gumballs will result in a new set of data, such as that shown in Table 1-6.2. Study the data, and plot this supply of Gumballs on the graph in Figure 1-6.1. Label the new supply curve $S_1$ and answer the questions below.

*Table 1-6.2*
NEW SUPPLY OF GUMBALLS: PART ONE

| Price (per Gumball) | Quantity supplied per week (number of Gumballs) |
|---|---|
| $0.15 | 0 |
| $0.20 | 50 |
| $0.25 | 100 |
| $0.30 | 150 |
| $0.35 | 200 |
| $0.40 | 250 |

2. Comparing the new supply curve ($S_1$) with the original supply curve (S), we can say that the change in the supply of Gumballs results in a shift of the supply curve to the (left/right). Such a shift indicates that at each of the possible prices shown, suppliers are now willing to offer a (smaller/larger) quantity; and at each of the possible quantities shown, suppliers are willing to accept a (higher/lower) minimum price. The cause of this supply curve shift was a(n) (increase/decrease) in prices of several of the raw materials used in making Gumballs.

Now, let's suppose that there is a dramatic change in the price of sugar, a resource used in the production of Gumballs. This change in the *ceteris paribus* conditions underlying the original supply of Gumballs will result in a new set of data shown in Table 1-6.3. Study the data, and plot this supply of Gumballs on the graph in Figure 1-6.1. Label the new supply curve $S_2$ and answer the questions that follow.

*Table 1-6.3*
### NEW SUPPLY OF GUMBALLS: PART TWO

| Price (per Gumball) | Quantity supplied per week (number of Gumballs) |
|---|---|
| $0.10 | 150 |
| $0.15 | 200 |
| $0.20 | 250 |
| $0.25 | 300 |
| $0.30 | 350 |
| $0.35 | 400 |

3. Comparing the new supply curve ($S_2$) with the original supply curve (S), we can say that the change in the supply of Gumballs results in a shift of the supply curve to the (left/right). Such a shift indicates that at each of the possible prices shown, suppliers are now willing to offer a (smaller/larger) quantity; and at each of the possible quantities shown, suppliers are willing to accept a (lower/higher) minimum price. The cause of this supply curve shift is a(n) (increase/decrease) in the price of sugar, a resource used in the production of Gumballs.

## Part B: Do You Get It?

Now, to check your understanding, choose the answer you think is the one best alternative in each of the following multiple-choice questions.

4.  All other things held constant, which of the following would *not* cause a change in the supply of beef?

    (A) A decrease in the price of beef (This will cause a decrease in the quantity supplied of beef.)

    (B) A decrease in the price of cattle feed

    (C) An increase in the price of cattle feed

    (D) An increase in the price of chickens

    (E) An increase in the cost of transporting cattle to market

5.  "Falling oil prices have caused a sharp decrease in the supply of oil." Speaking precisely, and using terms as they are defined by economists, choose the statement that best describes this quotation.

    (A) The quotation is correct: decrease in price causes a decrease in supply.

    (B) The quotation is incorrect: decrease in price causes an increase in supply, not a decrease in supply.

    (C) The quotation is incorrect: decrease in supply will cause falling prices.

    (D) The quotation is incorrect: decrease in price causes an increase in the quantity supplied, not a decrease in supply.

    (E) The quotation is incorrect: a decrease in price causes a decrease in the quantity supplied, not a decrease in supply.

6.  You overhear a fellow student say, "Economic markets are confusing. If supply increases, then price decreases; but if price decreases, then supply also will decrease. If supply falls, price will rise; but if price rises, supply also will rise." Dispel your friend's obvious confusion (in no more than one short paragraph) below.

## Part C: Producer Surplus

Once we have the supply curve, we can define the concept of *producer surplus*. Producer surplus is the value a producer receives from the sale of a good in excess of the marginal cost of producing the good. Stated differently, producer surplus is the difference between the price a seller receives for a unit of the good and the cost to the seller of producing that unit. For example, if your cost of producing a coat is $50 but you are able to sell the coat for $70, you have a producer surplus of $20.

Refer again to the supply curve data from Table 1-6.1, and assume the price is $0.25. Some sellers will benefit because based on their low marginal costs of production, they are willing to accept prices lower than $0.25 for this good. Note that each time the price is increased by $0.05, sellers will provide an additional 50 units. Table 1-6.4 shows how to calculate the producer surplus resulting from the price of $0.25.

*Table 1-6.4*
**FINDING THE PRODUCER SURPLUS WHEN THE PRICE IS $0.25**

| Price willing to accept | Quantity supplied | Producer surplus from the increments of 50 units if P = $0.25 |
|---|---|---|
| $0.10 | 50 units | ($0.15)(50 units) = $7.50 |
| $0.15 | 100 units | ($0.10)(50 units) = $5.00 |
| $0.20 | 150 units | ($0.05)(50 units) = $2.50 |
| $0.25 | 200 units | ($0.00)(50 units) = $0.00 |

The price for each unit is $0.25. For those producers willing to sell 50 units at a price of $0.10, the producer surplus for each unit is $0.15 (= $0.25-$0.10), making the producer surplus for all these units equal to $7.50.

There are other producers who will put an extra 50 units on the market if the price is $0.15. The producer surplus for these sellers is $0.10 per unit (= $0.25-$0.15) or a total of $5.00 for all 50 units.

If the price is raised another $0.05 to $0.20, an extra 50 units will be supplied; the producer surplus for these units is $2.50, or $0.05 per unit (= $0.25-$0.20).

If the price is $0.25, another 50 units will be supplied. The producer surplus for these units, however, is $0.00 since $0.25 is the lowest price these producers are willing to accept. Thus, if the price is $0.25, a total of 200 units are supplied and the total producer surplus is $15.00.

## Part D: Calculating Consumer Surplus Using a Graph

An approximation of the total producer surplus from a given number of units of a good can be shown graphically as the area above the supply curve and below the price paid for those units.

In Figure 1-6.2, redraw the supply curve (S) from the data in Table 1-6.1. We see that if the price is $0.25, the quantity supplied is 200 units. Consumer surplus from these 200 units is the shaded area between the supply curve S and the horizontal price line at $0.25. We can find the area of this triangle using the familiar rule of (½) × base × height.

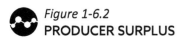

*Figure 1-6.2*
PRODUCER SURPLUS

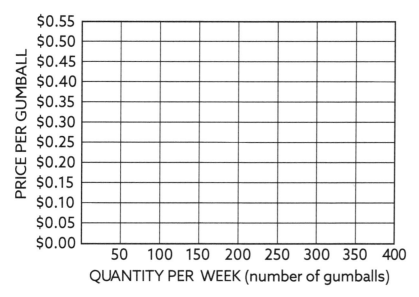

7. What is the value of producer surplus in this market if the price is $0.25? _____

   Write the equation showing how you calculated the value of the area of the triangle representing producer surplus.

8. Answer these questions based on the discussion of Figure 1-6.2.

   (A) If the price is increased from $0.25 to $0.30, producer surplus will (increase/decrease). Why?

   (B) If the price is decreased from $0.25 to $0.20, producer surplus will (increase/decrease). Why?

# Reasons for Changes in Supply

## Part A: Does the Supply Curve Shift?

Read the eight newspaper headlines in Table 1-6.5, and use the table to record the impact of each event on the supply of cars from U.S. auto producers. In the second column, indicate whether the event in the headline will cause American auto producers to provide more or less cars. Use the third column to indicate whether there is a change in supply ($\Delta S$) or a change in quantity supplied ($\Delta Qs$) of cars. In the fourth column, decide whether the supply curve shifts to the right or left or does not shift. Finally, in the last column draw and label the graph showing the shift in the curve for U.S.-made autos.

*Table 1-6.5*
**IMPACT OF EVENTS ON SUPPLY OF U.S.-MADE AUTOS**

| Headline | Should U.S. auto firms produce more or less? | Is there a change in supply ($\Delta S$) or a change in quantity supplied ($\Delta Qs$)? | Does the supply curve of cars shift to the right or left or not shift? | Draw and label the graph showing the shift in the curve. |
|---|---|---|---|---|
| 1. Auto Workers' Union Agrees to Wage Cuts | More / Less | $\Delta S$ / $\Delta Qs$ | Right / Left / No Shift | |
| 2. New Robot Technology Increases Efficiency | More / Less | $\Delta S$ / $\Delta Qs$ | Right / Left / No Shift | |
| 3. Price of U.S. Cars Increases | More / Less | $\Delta S$ / $\Delta Qs$ | Right / Left / No Shift | |
| 4. Nationwide Auto Workers Strike Begins | More / Less | $\Delta S$ / $\Delta Qs$ | Right / Left / No Shift | |
| 5. Cost of Steel Decreases | More / Less | $\Delta S$ / $\Delta Qs$ | Right / Left / No Shift | |
| 6. Major Auto Producer Goes Out of Business | More / Less | $\Delta S$ / $\Delta Qs$ | Right / Left / No Shift | |
| 7. Buyers Reject New Car Models | More / Less | $\Delta S$ / $\Delta Qs$ | Right / Left / No Shift | |
| 8. Government Gives Car Producers a Subsidy | More / Less | $\Delta S$ / $\Delta Qs$ | Right / Left / No Shift | |

## Part B: Why Does the Supply Curve Shift?

Categorize each change in supply in Part A according to the reason why supply changed. In Table 1-6.6, place an X next to the reason that the headline indicated a change in supply. In some cases, more than one headline could be matched to a reason. It is possible a headline does not indicate a shift in supply because it will result in a change in quantity supplied rather than a change in supply.

*Table 1-6.6*
**IMPACT OF EVENTS ON SUPPLY OF U.S.-MADE AUTOS**

|  | Headline number | | | | | | | |
|---|---|---|---|---|---|---|---|---|
| Reason | 1 | 2 | 3 | 4 | 5 | 6 | 7 | 8 |
| 9. A change in costs of inputs (steel and other metals) to production process |  |  |  |  |  |  |  |  |
| 10. A change in technology |  |  |  |  |  |  |  |  |
| 11. A change in the number of producers in the market |  |  |  |  |  |  |  |  |
| 12. Government policies |  |  |  |  |  |  |  |  |

# Equilibrium Price and Equilibrium Quantity

Table 1-7.1 below shows both the demand for gumballs and the supply of gumballs. Plot these data on the graph in Figure 1-7.1. Label the demand curve D and label the supply curve S. Then answer the questions that follow.

> Student Alert: A "change in demand" or a "change in supply" results in a change in price, while a "change in quantity demanded" or a "change in quantity supplied" is the result of a change in price. (!)

*Table 1-7.1*
**DEMAND FOR AND SUPPLY OF GUMBALLS**

| Price (per Gumball) | Quantity demanded (millions of Gumballs) | Quantity supplied (millions of Gumballs) |
|---|---|---|
| $0.05 | 400 | 0 |
| $0.10 | 350 | 50 |
| $0.15 | 300 | 100 |
| $0.20 | 250 | 150 |
| $0.25 | 200 | 200 |
| $0.30 | 150 | 250 |
| $0.35 | 100 | 300 |
| $0.40 | 50 | 350 |
| $0.45 | 0 | 400 |

*Figure 1-7.1*
**DEMAND FOR AND SUPPLY OF GUMBALLS**

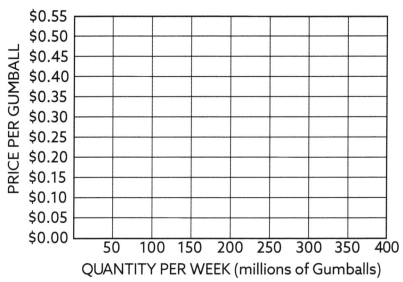

1. Under these conditions, competitive market forces would tend to establish an equilibrium price of $ _____ per Gumball and an equilibrium quantity of _____.

2. If the price currently prevailing in the market is $0.30 per Gumball, buyers would want to buy _____ Gumballs and sellers would want to sell _____ Gumballs. Under these conditions, there would be a (shortage/surplus) of _____ gumballs. Competitive market forces would cause the price to (increase/decrease) to a price of _____ per Gumball. At this new price, buyers would now want to buy _____ Gumballs, and sellers now want to sell _____ Gumballs. Because of this change in (price/underlying conditions), the (demand/quantity demanded) (increased/decreased) by _____ Gumballs, and the (supply/quantity supplied) (increased/decreased) by _____ Gumballs.

3. If the price currently prevailing in the market is $0.20 per Gumball, buyers would want to buy _____ Gumballs, and sellers would want to sell _____ Gumballs. Under these conditions, there would be a (shortage/surplus) of _____ Gumballs. Competitive market forces would cause the price to (increase/decrease) to a price of _____ per Gumball. At this new price, buyers would now want to buy _____ Gumballs, and sellers now want to sell _____ Gumballs. Because of this change in (price/underlying conditions), the (demand/quantity demanded) (increased/decreased) by _____ Gumballs, and the (supply/quantity supplied) (increased/decreased) by _____ Gumballs.

4. At equilibrium, is each of the following true or false? Explain.

   (A) The quantity demanded is equal to the quantity supplied.

   (B) Demand equals supply.

# UNIT 1 ACTIVITY 1-7.1 (continued)

5. Now, suppose a mysterious blight causes the supply schedule for Gumballs to change as shown in Table 1-7.2:

*Table 1-7.2*
**NEW SUPPLY OF GUMBALLS**

| Price (per Gumball) | Quantity supplied (millions of Gumballs) |
|---|---|
| $0.15 | 0 |
| $0.20 | 50 |
| $0.25 | 100 |
| $0.30 | 150 |
| $0.35 | 200 |

Plot the new supply schedule on the axes in Figure 1-7.2 and label it $S_1$. Label the new equilibrium $E_1$.

*Figure 1-7.2*
**DEMAND FOR AND SUPPLY FOR GUMBALLS**

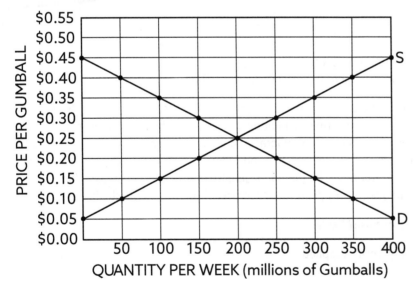

Under these conditions, competitive market forces would tend to establish an equilibrium price of _____ per Gumball and an equilibrium quantity of _____ Gumballs.

Compared with the equilibrium price in Question 1, we say that because of this change in (price/underlying conditions), the (supply/quantity supplied) changed; and both the equilibrium price and the equilibrium quantity changed. The equilibrium price (increased/decreased), and the equilibrium quantity (increased/decreased).

---

AP Macroeconomics Student Workbook © Council for Economic Education, New York, NY

6.  Now, with the supply schedule at $S_1$, suppose further that a sharp drop in people's incomes as the result of a prolonged recession causes the demand schedule to change as shown in Table 1-7.3.

*Table 1-7.3*
**NEW DEMAND FOR GUMBALLS**

| Price (per Gumball) | Quantity supplied (millions of Gumballs) |
| --- | --- |
| $0.15 | 200 |
| $0.20 | 150 |
| $0.25 | 100 |
| $0.30 | 50 |
| $0.35 | 0 |

Plot the new demand schedule on the axes in Figure 1-7.3 and label it $D_1$. Label the new equilibrium $E_2$.

*Figure 1-7.3*
**DEMAND FOR AND SUPPLY FOR GUMBALLS**

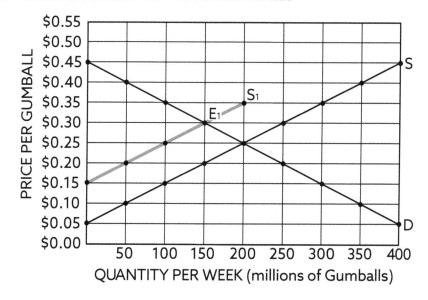

Under these conditions, with the supply schedule at $S_1$, competitive market forces would establish an equilibrium price of _____ per gumball and an equilibrium quantity of _____ gumballs. Compared with the equilibrium price in Question 5, because of this change in (price/underlying conditions), the (demand/quantity demanded) changed. The equilibrium price (increased/decreased), and the equilibrium quantity (increased/decreased).

# Shifts in Supply and Demand

## Part A: The Market for Jelly Beans

Fill in the blanks with the letter of the graph that illustrates each situation. You may use a graph more than once.

*Figure 1-7.4*
**THE SUPPLY AND DEMAND FOR JELLY BEANS**

Graph A

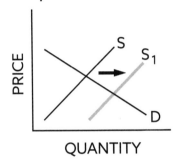

Graph B

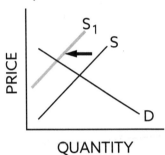

Graph C

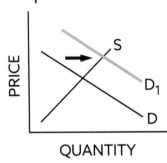

Graph D

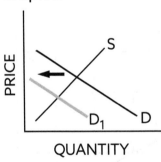

1. The price of sugar, a key ingredient in producing jelly beans, increases. ____

2. The price of bubble gum, a close substitute for jelly beans, increases. ____

3. A machine is invented that makes jelly beans at a lower cost. ____

4. The government places a tax on foreign jelly beans, which have a considerable share of the market. ____

5. The price of soda, a complementary good for jelly beans, increases. ____

6. Widespread prosperity allows people to buy more jelly beans. ____

## Part B: Apples, Pears, and Pies

Circle the words that show the effects on price and quantity for each situation and complete the graphs below. Then provide your reasoning.

1. Apples in Boston

   Connecticut ships large amounts of apples to all parts of the United States by rail. A hurricane destroys most of Connecticut.

   Price:        Rises/Unchanged/Falls

   Quantity:    Rises/Unchanged/Falls

   Reason:

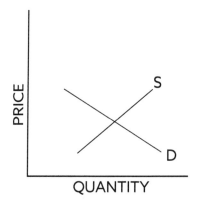

2. What happens to the price of land devoted to apple orchards in the state of Washington?

   Price:        Rises/Unchanged/Falls

   Quantity:    Rises/Unchanged/Falls

   Reason:

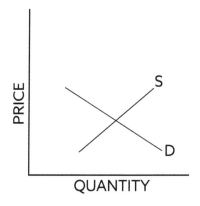

3. What happens to the market for Apples grown in the state of Washington? Remember, there are no apples being shipped out of Connecticut.

   Price:        Rises/Unchanged/Falls

   Quantity:    Rises/Unchanged/Falls

   Reason:

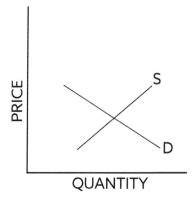

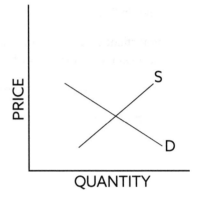

4.  What happens to the market for pears?

    Price:        Rises/Unchanged/Falls

    Quantity:    Rises/Unchanged/Falls

    Reason:

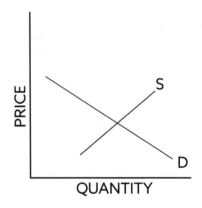

5.  What happens to the market for Apple pies?

    Price:        Rises/Unchanged/Falls

    Quantity:    Rises/Unchanged/Falls

    Reason:

# UNIT 1 **ACTIVITY 1-SA.1**

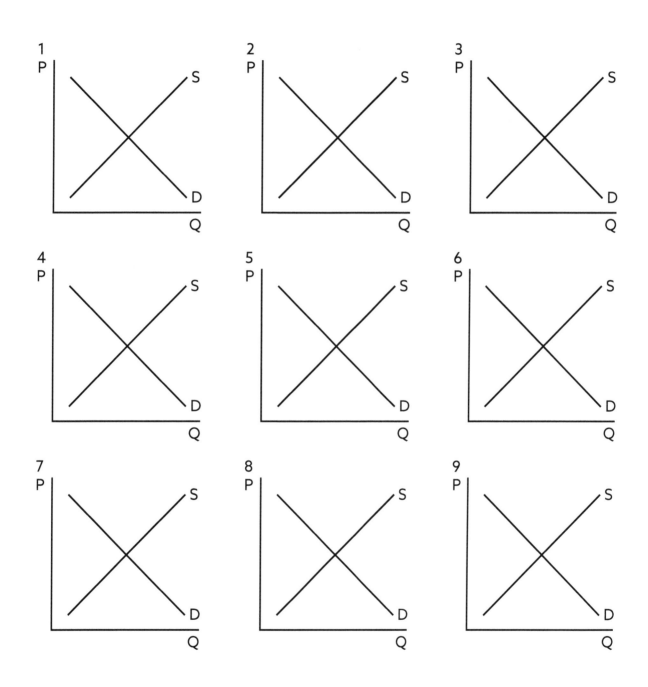

**Directions:** Graph each situation. ***Show the proper shift and identify the equilibrium price and quantity and the new equilibrium price and quantity.***

**Supply:** Graph each situation. ***Show the proper shift and identify the equilibrium price and quantity and the new equilibrium price and quantity.***

1. **New technology:** Draw a graph that depicts the market in solar panels. A manufacturer of solar panels invests in new technology that reduces the cost of production.

2. **Input prices:** Draw a graph that depicts the market for orange juice. A freeze in Florida destroys much of the orange crop, causing the price of oranges to rise.

3. **Changes in government policies:** Draw a graph that depicts the market for cigarettes. A new government regulation imposes higher taxes on cigarette manufacturers.

4. **Changes in the price of related goods:** Draw a graph that depicts the market for lemonade. The price of frozen lemonade-flavored ice pops increases. What happens to the supply of lemonade?

5. **Seller expectations of the future:** Draw a graph that depicts the current market for tires. A manufacturer of automobile tires notices that due to a drought the supply of rubber will definitely decrease in the future. The company decides to put fewer tires on the market today, waiting for the price to increase.

6. **Changes in technology:** Draw a graph that depicts the market for sneakers. A new type of manufacturing equipment reduces the time and cost of producing sneakers.

7. **Changes in the availability of resources:** Draw a graph that depicts the market for tuna fish sandwiches. A fishing ban is implemented to protect a certain species of tuna.

8. **Changes in the price of inputs:** Draw a graph that depicts the market for cars. The price of steel, a major input in the production of cars, increases due to a trade dispute with a major steel producer.

9. **Changes in government subsidies:** Draw a graph that depicts the market for popcorn. The government increases subsidies for corn farmers.

10. **Changes in the number of suppliers:** Draw a graph that depicts the market for organic food. A new entrant into the market for organic food increases competition.

11. **Technology:** Draw a graph that depicts the market for T-shirts. A clothing manufacturer invests in new machinery that allows for faster production of clothes.

12. **Input prices:** Draw a graph that depicts the market for ice cream. Due to a shortage of milk, the cost of producing ice cream increases.

13. **Government policies:** Draw a graph that depicts the market for electric cars. A government implements a subsidy on electric cars, reducing the cost of production for electric cars.

14. **Technology:** Draw a graph that depicts the market for coffee. A coffee shop invests in new equipment that allows for faster preparation of coffee drinks.

15. **Change in the number of suppliers:** Draw a graph that depicts the market for hamburgers. The diner in a small town goes out of business.

**Demand:** Graph each situation. *Show the proper shift and identify the equilibrium price and quantity and the new equilibrium price and quantity.*

16. **Changes in income – normal good:** Draw a graph that depicts the market for concert tickets. An increase in the minimum wage leads to an increase in the disposable income for working teenagers.

17. **Changes in the number of buyers:** Draw a graph that depicts the market for healthcare in Florida. A large number of baby boomers retire and move to Florida.

18. **Changes in consumer tastes and preferences:** Draw a graph that depicts the market for Brand A headphones . A popular celebrity starts endorsing Brand B headphones.

19. **Changes in the price of related goods – substitutes:** Draw a graph that depicts the market for butter. The price of margarine increases.

20. **Changes in consumer tastes and preferences:** Draw a graph that depicts the market for broccoli. Doctors announce that healthy eating leads to clear skin and taller children.

21. **Changes in consumer tastes and preferences:** Draw a graph that depicts the market for gym membership. Video shorts aimed at teenagers and the under-30 crowd show people working out and showing off muscles and lean body masses.

22. **Changes in income – inferior good:** Draw a graph that depicts the market for "store-brand' grocery items. A recession leads to high unemployment.

23. **Change in consumer expectations of future price:** Draw a graph that depicts the market for coffee. People expect the price of coffee to rise in the future due to political unrest in South America.

24. **Change in the price of related goods – complements:** Draw a graph that depicts the market for cell phone chargers. The demand for cell phones decreases. Cell phones and chargers are bought together.

25. **Change in the number of buyers:** Draw a graph that depicts the market for beer. The drinking age in the United States is raised to 25 years old.

# UNIT 2
## MEASURING ECONOMIC PERFORMANCE

# UNIT 2 **MACROECONOMICS KEY IDEAS**

- **Macroeconomics** is the study of the economy as a whole; microeconomics is the study of individual parts of the economy such as businesses, households, and prices.

- Macroeconomics looks at the forest while microeconomics looks at the trees.

- A **circular flow** diagram illustrates the major flows of goods and services, resources, and income in an economy. It shows how changes in these flows can alter the level of goods and services, employment, and income.

- **Gross domestic product (GDP)** is the market value of all final goods and services produced in a nation in one year. It is the most important measure of production and output.

- GDP is a useful indicator of a nation's economic performance, but it has some limitations, such as failing to account for nonmarket transactions.

- GDP may be calculated three ways:

    1. **The expenditures approach**: add all the consumption, investment, government expenditures, and net exports

        GDP = C + I + G + Xn.

    2. **The income approach**: add all the income received by owners of resources (land, labor, capital, entrepreneurship) in the economy.

        Total Income (wages, rents, profits, interest) + Taxes on production and imports (indirect Business taxes) + Consumption of fixed capital/Depreciation - net foreign factor income
        + Statistical discrepancies

    3. **The value added approach**:
        Value Added Approach = The Value of all Final Goods and Services produced in the economy - the value of intermediate goods and services used to produce the final goods.

- **The expenditures approach** to calculating GDP counts only final goods and services to avoid double counting. That is, it does not count intermediate goods and services.

- The **expenditures approach** to calculating GDP does not count the purchase of secondhand goods, stocks and bonds, because these do not represent new production during the year. GDP also does not include items purchased in illegal markets.

- The **income approach** to calculating GDP includes profits and income earned by foreigners in the United States but does not count income and profits earned by U.S. citizens abroad, transfer payments like Social Security, unemployment compensation, or certain interest payments.

- If domestic prices increase relative to prices in other countries, imports will increase while exports decrease because people want to purchase the goods and services where they are relatively cheaper.

- **Nominal GDP** measures aggregate output using current prices. **Real GDP** measures aggregate output using constant prices, thus removing the effect of changes in the overall price level.

- **Inflation** is a general increase in the price level in the economy. Savers, lenders, and people on fixed incomes generally are hurt by unanticipated inflation. Borrowers gain from unanticipated inflation.

- **Price indices** measure price changes in the economy. They are used to compare the prices of a given bundle or "market basket" of goods and services in one year with the prices of the same bundle/market basket in another year.

- The most frequently used price index is the **Consumer Price Index (CPI)**.

- Price changes over time are measured by comparing prices each year to the prices in a selected year, called the base year. The price level in the base year has an index number of 100. The price level in other years is expressed in relation to the price level in the base year.

- Unexpected inflation arbitrarily redistributes wealth from one group of individuals to another group, such as lenders to borrowers.

- **The labor force** is defined as people who have a job (employed) and people who are not working but are actively seeking a job (unemployed). The labor force participation rate is the percentage of the population over the age of 16 that is in the labor force.

- Unemployment occurs when people who are willing and able to work are not working. The unemployment rate equals the number of people who are not working but who are actively seeking a job as a percentage of the labor force.

- There are three types of unemployment: **frictional**, **cyclical**, and **structural**.

- The unemployment rate associated with full employment is above zero because frictional and structural unemployment will always exist. **Full employment** occurs where cyclical unemployment equals zero.

- The **natural rate of unemployment** is the unemployment rate that would exist when the economy produces full-employment real output. It is equal to the sum of frictional and structural unemployment.

- The phases of the **business cycle** are contraction, peak, recession, and trough.

- The difference between actual output and potential output is the **output gap**. Potential output is also called full-employment output. It is the level of GDP where unemployment is equal to the natural rate of unemployment.

# Understanding the Circular Flow of the Macroeconomy

Identify which of the following terms belongs in each of the numbered blanks in the circular flow diagram and fill in the blanks.

Taxes

Saving

Investment

Exports

Government spending

Imports

Payments for goods and services

Income (rent/wages/interest/profit)

Revenue from selling goods and services

Leakage

Injection

Payments for resources (rent/wages/interest/profit)

## The Circular Flow of Resources, Goods, Services, and Money Payments

Money that flows out of the Circular Flow 1. _____

$

Product market
(goods and services)

$

Government
Inflow:    4. _____
Outflow:  5. _____

Households (resource owners)
Inflow:    2. _____
Outflow: 3. _____

Financial institutions
Inflow:    6. _____
Outflow:  7. _____

Firms (producers)
Inflow:   10. _____
Outflow: 11. _____

International sector
Inflow:    8. _____
Outflow:  9. _____

Factor market
(Resources: land, labor, capital, entrepreneurial skill)

$

$

Money that flows into the Circular Flow 12. _____

# The Expenditures Approach to GDP

## Part A: Expenditures Approach: Is This Counted as Part of GDP?

Determine if each of the following is included or excluded when calculating GDP. Briefly explain why.

1.  A monthly check received by an economics student who has been granted a government scholarship

2.  A farmer's purchase of a new tractor

3.  A plumber's purchase of a two-year-old used truck

4.  Cashing a U.S. government bond

5.  The services of a barber cutting his own hair

6.  A Social Security check from the government to a retired sales associate

7.  Chevrolet's purchase of tires to put on the cars they are producing

8.  The government's purchase of a new submarine for the Navy

9.  A barber's income from cutting hair

10. Income received from the sale of Nike stock

## Part B: GDP: Is It Counted and Where? Expenditure Approach

For each of the following examples, write one of the following in the space provided:

**C**   if the item is counted as consumption spending.

**I**   if the item is counted as investment spending.

**G**   if the item is counted as government spending.

**Xn** if the item is counted as net exports.

**NC** if the item is not counted in GDP.

_____ 11. You spend $15.00 to see a movie.

_____ 12. A family pays a contractor $450,000 for a house he built for them this year.

_____ 13. A family pays $275,000 for a house built thirty years ago.

_____ 14. An accountant pays a tailor $175 to sew a suit for her.

_____ 15. The government increases its defense expenditures by $1,000,000,000.

_____ 16. The government makes a $1,500 Social Security payment to a retired person.

_____ 17. You purchase $1,000 worth of McDonald's stock.

_____ 18. At the end of a year, a flour-milling firm finds that its inventories of grain and flour are $100,000 higher than its inventories at the beginning of the year.

_____ 19. Parents work hard caring for their two children.

_____ 20. Ford Motor Company buys new auto-making robots.

_____ 21. You pay $1800 a month to rent an apartment.

_____ 22. Consumer electronics corporation Apple Inc. builds a new factory in the United States.

_____ 23. Mondelēz International purchases the Nabisco company.

_____ 24. You buy a new Toyota that was made in Japan.

_____ 25. You pay tuition to attend college.

# Three Approaches for Calculating GDP

Econo Island produces tomatoes and tomato soup, but nothing else. Some of the tomatoes are consumed domestically, some are exported, and some are used to make soup. Some cans of soup are consumed domestically and some are exported. All ingredients for making soup are imported except for tomatoes. Labor is the only factor of production on Econo Island. The government of Econo Island purchases soup to supplement the public schools' lunch program.

Consider the following data:

| Data from Tomato Factories | |
|---|---|
| Total labor hours worked: | 200,000 hours |
| Tomato factory wage: | $6/hour |
| Total pounds of tomatoes sold: | 240,000 lbs. |
| Price per pound of tomatoes: | $5 per lb. |
| **Data from Soup Factories** | |
| Total labor hours worked: | 75,000 hours |
| Soup factory wage: | $12/hour |
| Total pounds of non-tomato ingredient inputs: | 80,000 lbs. |
| Price of non-tomato ingredients: | $2.50/lb. |
| Total tomato inputs: | 60,000 tomatoes |
| Total tomato soup sales: | 140,000 cans |
| Price of soup per can: | $10/can |
| **Data from Households** | |
| Tomatoes consumed: | 160,000 lbs. |
| Cans of soup consumed: | 120,000 cans |
| **Government Data** | |
| Soup purchased by government: | 10,000 cans of soup |
| **Trade Data** | |
| Soup exported: | 10,000 cans |
| Tomatoes exported: | 20,000 lbs. tomatoes |
| Ingredients imported: | 80,000 lbs. |

1. First, calculate GDP using the income approach.

2. Now we will use the expenditure approach to calculate GDP.

   (A) Find the total consumer spending.

   (B) Find the total government spending.

   (C) Find the total spending on export goods.

   (D) Find the total spending on imported goods.

   (E) Find the GDP.

3. Now calculate GDP using the value added approach.

   (A) What is the total value added by the tomato factories?

   (B) What is the total value added by the soup factories?

   (C) What is the GDP?

4. The country of Econo Island has a population of 100 people. What is the country's GDP per capita?

# UNIT 2 ACTIVITY 2-3.1

## Calculating Price Indices

$$\text{Price Index} = \frac{\text{Current-year cost*}}{\text{Base year cost*}} \times 100$$

Assume an average consumer buys only three items, as shown in Table 2-3.1.

*Table 2-3.1*
**PRICES OF THREE GOODS COMPARED WITH BASE-YEAR PRICE**

| | Quantity bought in base year | Unit price in base year | Spending in base year | Unit price in Year 1 | Spending in Year 1 | Unit price in Year 2 | Spending in Year 2 |
|---|---|---|---|---|---|---|---|
| Whole pizza | 30 | $5.00 | | $7.00 | | $9.00 | |
| Flash drive | 40 | $6.00 | | $5.00 | | $4.00 | |
| Six-pack of soda | 60 | $1.50 | | $2.00 | | $2.50 | |
| Total | – | – | | – | | – | |

Fill in the blanks in Table 2-3.1.

1. How much would $100 of goods and services purchased in the base year cost in Year 1? Show your work.

The rate of change in this index is determined by looking at the percentage change from one year to the next. If, for example, the CPI were 150 in one year and 165 the next, then the year-to-year percentage change is 10 percent. You can compute the change using this formula:

$$\text{Rate of Inflation} = \frac{\text{Change in CPI}}{\text{Beginning CPI}} \times 100$$

2. What was the percentage increase in prices in this case? Show your calculations.

3. What is the percentage increase in prices from the base year to Year 2? _____ Show your work.

*Table 2-3.2*
## CONSTRUCTING A PRICE INDEX

| Basic market basket item | No. of units | Year 1 Price per unit | Year 1 Cost of market basket | Year 2 Price per unit | Year 2 Cost of market basket | Year 3 Price per unit | Year 3 Cost of market basket |
|---|---|---|---|---|---|---|---|
| Cheese | 2 lbs. | $1.75 | | $1.50 | $3.00 | $1.50 | |
| Blue jeans | 2 pair | $12.00 | $24.00 | $15.50 | | $20.00 | $40.00 |
| Gasoline | 10 gals. | $1.25 | | $1.60 | $16.00 | $2.70 | |
| Total | – | – | | – | | – | |

Fill in the blanks in Table 2-3.2.

4. If Year 2 is selected as the base year, calculate the price index for each year. Show your work.

   (A) Year 1 = _____

   (B) Year 2 = _____

   (C) Year 3 = _____

5. These price indices indicate that there was a 40 percent increase in prices between Year 2 and Year 3.

   (A) What is the percentage increase between Year 1 and Year 2? _____.

   (B) What is the percentage increase between Year 1 and Year 3? _____.

# Real versus Nominal Values

## Converting Nominal GDP to Real GDP

To use GDP to measure output growth, it must be converted from nominal to real. Let's say nominal GDP in Year 1 is $1,000 and in Year 2 it is $1,100. Does this mean the economy has grown 10 percent between Year 1 and Year 2? Not necessarily. If prices have risen, part of the increase in nominal GDP in Year 2 will represent the increase in prices. GDP that has been adjusted for price changes is called real GDP. If GDP isn't adjusted for price changes, we call it nominal GDP.

To compute real GDP in a given year, use the following formula: *Real GDP = nominal GDP/(price index/100).*

To compute real output growth in GDP from one year to another, subtract real GDP for Year 2 from real GDP in Year 1. Divide the answer (the change in real GDP from the previous year) by real GDP in Year 1. The result, multiplied by 100, is the percentage growth in real GDP from Year 1 to Year 2. (If real GDP declines from Year 1 to Year 2, the answer will be a negative percentage.) Here's the formula:

$$\text{Output growth} = \frac{(\text{real GDP in Year 2} - \text{real GDP in Year 1})}{\text{real GDP in Year 1}} \times 100.$$

For example, if real GDP in Year 1 = $1,000 and in Year 2 = $1,028, then the output growth rate from Year 1 to Year 2 is 2.8%: (1,028-1,000)/1,000 = .028, which we multiply by 100 in order to express the result as a percentage.

To understand the impact of output changes, we usually look at real GDP per capita. To do so, we divide the real GDP of any period by a country's average population during the same period. This procedure enables us to determine how much of the output growth of a country simply went to supply the increase in population and how much of the growth represented improvements in the standard of living of the entire population. In our example, let's say the population in Year 1 was 100 and in Year 2 it was 110. What was real GDP per capita in Years 1 and 2?

Year 1
$$\text{Real GDP per capita} = \frac{\text{Year 1 real GDP}}{\text{population in Year 1}} = \frac{\$1,000}{100} = \$10.$$

Year 2
$$\text{Real GDP per capita} = \frac{\$1,028}{110} = \$9.30.$$

In this example, real GDP per capita fell even though output growth was positive. Developing countries with positive output growth but high rates of population growth often experience this condition.

Use the information in Table 2-3.3 to answer the following questions.

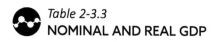
*Table 2-3.3*
**NOMINAL AND REAL GDP**

|        | Nominal GDP | Price index | Population |
|--------|-------------|-------------|------------|
| Year 3 | $5,000      | 125         | 11         |
| Year 4 | $6,600      | 150         | 12         |

6. What is the real GDP in Year 3? _____

7. What is the real GDP in Year 4? _____

8. What is the real GDP per capita in Year 3? _____

9. What is the real GDP per capita in Year 4? _____

10. What is the rate of real output growth between Years 3 and 4?

11. What is the rate of real output growth per capita between Years 3 and 4?

12. Explain one limitation of using nominal GDP.

# Anticipated versus Unanticipated Inflation

Student Alert: Inflation is an increase in
the price level in the economy. It does not
necessarily mean that the price of every good
is going up!

## Who Is Hurt and Who Is Helped by Unanticipated Inflation?

Identify whether each of the following examples leads to a person or group being hurt or helped by unanticipated
inflation. Circle your response and explain your answer.

**H** – the person or group is hurt by unanticipated inflation
**G** – the person or group gains from unanticipated inflation
**U** – it is uncertain if the person or group is affected by unanticipated inflation

1.  Banks extend many fixed-rate loans. H G U

    Explain:


2.  A farmer buys machinery with a fixed-rate loan to be repaid over a ten-year period. H G U

    Explain:


3.  Your savings from your summer job are in a savings account paying a fixed rate of interest. H G U

    Explain:


4.  An elderly couple living off fixed retirement payments of $2,000 a month. H G U

    Explain:


5.  The federal government has a $14 trillion debt. H G U

    Explain:


6.  A firm signs a contract to provide maintenance services at a fixed rate for the next five years. H G U

    Explain:


7.  A state government receives revenue mainly from an income tax. H G U

    Explain:

8.  A local government receives revenue mainly from fixed-rate license fees charged to businesses. H G U

    Explain:

9.  Your friend rents an apartment with a three-year lease. H G U

    Explain:

10. A bank has loaned millions of dollars for home mortgages at a fixed rate of interest. H G U

    Explain:

11. Parents are putting savings for their child's college education in a bank savings account. H G U

    Explain:

12. Your boss gives you a 5% raise, but unanticipated inflation is 8%. H G  U

    Explain:

# The Costs of Inflation

For each situation, place an X in the box representing the cost of inflation that is best represented.

| Situation | Shoe leather costs | Menu costs | Unit of account costs |
|---|---|---|---|
| (A) Your favorite local restaurant raises its prices and has to print new advertisements. | | | |
| (B) Workers in Germany in 1922 are paid and shop three times a day due to hyperinflation. | | | |
| (C) You have to change your automatic bill payment in your online banking account because the rent for your apartment went up. | | | |
| (D) You remember when the price of gasoline was $1.25 per gallon. | | | |
| (E) You work at your local grocery store and place new higher price stickers on the store's shelves. | | | |
| (F) Your weekly grocery bill increases, but the amount of groceries you purchase does not. | | | |

# Measuring Unemployment

*The labor force participation rate* (LFPR) is defined as the percentage of the population that is considered part of the labor force.

$$\text{LFPR} = \frac{\text{labor force}}{\text{population}} \times 100.$$

*The unemployment rate* (UR) is defined as the number of people who are unemployed as a percentage of the labor force.

$$\text{UR} = \frac{\text{number of unemployed}}{\text{labor force}} \times 100.$$

> Student Alert: The LFPR is the labor force as a percentage of the population. The UR is the number of people unemployed as a percentage of the labor force. Make sure to use the right denominator.

1. Fill in the last three columns of Table 2-5.1. All of the population and labor-force data are in millions.

Table 2-5.1
**CIVILIAN EMPLOYMENT**

| Year | Civilian non-institutional population age 16 and over | Civilian labor force | | | UR | LFPR |
| --- | --- | --- | --- | --- | --- | --- |
| | | Employed | Unemployed | Total | | |
| 1980 | 137 | 79 | 4 | | | |
| 1990 | 168 | 99 | 8 | | | |
| 2000 | 188 | 117 | 7 | | | |
| 2010 | 209 | 135 | 6 | | | |
| April 2020 | 258 | 133 | 23 | | | |

# Classifying Types of Unemployment Solutions

For each of the following situations, put the appropriate letter before the example.

**F** – if it is an example of frictional unemployment.

**C** – if it is an example of cyclical unemployment.

**S** – if it is an example of structural unemployment.

**N** – if it is an example of someone who is not counted as unemployed.

____ 1.   A computer programmer is laid off because of a recession.

____ 2.   A literary editor leaves her job in New York to look for a new job in San Francisco.

____ 3.   A college graduate works at a job that does not require a college education.

____ 4.   An unemployed high school graduate is looking for his first job.

____ 5.   An electrician quits their job because they are tired of dealing with the long commute to work.

____ 6.   Slumping sales lead to the cashier being laid off.

____ 7.   An individual refuses a Job because the salary is too low and keeps looking for a better paying job.

____ 8.   A high school drop-out lacks the skills necessary for a particular job.

____ 9.   Workers are laid off when the local manufacturing plant closes because the product made there isn't selling during a recession.

____ 10.  An assembly line worker becomes unemployed when a new machine does her job faster.

____ 11.  An individual has been laid off during a recession and has been looking for work unsuccessfully for so long that he has finally given up actively seeking a job.

____ 12.  Advances in technology make the newspaper delivery person's job obsolete.

# The Business Cycle

The *business cycle* refers to the ups and downs in an economy. In the short run, the economy alternates between upturns and downturns as measured by the three macroeconomic indicators.

1. Draw a graph of the business cycle using GDP as your measure of economic activity. Make sure that you label the horizontal and vertical axes correctly. Label the phases and high and low points.

2. On your graph, plot a point indicating where in the business cycle you think the economy is currently operating. Explain how you selected that location.

3. On your graph, shade and label the areas that represent the negative and positive output gaps.

4.  Draw a graph of a business cycle using unemployment as your measure of economic activity. That is, label the vertical axis with the unemployment rate. Make sure that you also label the horizontal axis. Label the phases of the business cycle on your graph. Remember that you are graphing the unemployment rate (rather than output) on your graph. Think about what happens to the unemployment rate during each phase of the business cycle!

# UNIT 3
## NATIONAL INCOME AND
## PRICE DETERMINATION

# UNIT 3 **MACROECONOMICS KEY IDEAS**

- **Aggregate demand** (AD) and **aggregate supply** (AS) curves look and operate much like the market supply and demand curves used in microeconomics. However, aggregate demand and aggregate supply curves depict somewhat different concepts, and they change for different reasons. AD and AS curves are used to illustrate changes in real output and the price level of an economy.

- The aggregate demand (AD) curve describes the relationship between the price level and the quantity of goods and services demanded by households (consumption), firms (investment), government (government spending), and the rest of the world (net exports).

- The negative slope of the AD curve is explained by the real wealth effect, the interest rate effect, and the exchange rate effect.

- Any change in the components of aggregate demand (consumption, investment, government spending, or net exports) that is not due to changes in the price level leads to a shift of the AD curve.

- The upward slope of the **short-run aggregate supply curve** (SRAS) is explained by fixed input costs (e.g., sticky wages). The **long-run aggregate supply** (LRAS) curve is vertical at the full-employment level of output.

- In the long run, in the absence of government policy actions, flexible wages and prices will adjust to restore full employment and unemployment will revert to its natural rate after a shock to aggregate demand or short-run aggregate supply.

- The **marginal propensity to consume** (MPC) is the additional consumption spending from an additional dollar of income. The **marginal propensity to save** (MPS) is the additional savings from an additional dollar of income:

  MPC + MPS = 1.

- The **spending multiplier** shows the relationship between changes in spending and the maximum resulting changes in real gross domestic product (GDP). The simple spending multiplier is given as:

$$\text{Spending multiplier} = \frac{1}{1 - \text{MPC}} = \frac{1}{\text{MPS}}.$$

- Shifts in AD can change the level of output, and the price level. The determinants of AD include: consumer spending, investment spending, government spending, and net exports.

- Shifts in SRAS can also change the level of output and the price level. The determinants of SRAS include: changes in input prices, productivity, actions of government (that affect businesses), and the quantity of available resources.

- There are two types of inflation: **demand pull inflation** and **cost-push inflation**. When high unemployment occurs along with high inflation, it is known as stagflation.

- In the short run, equilibrium levels of GDP can occur at less than, greater than, or at the full-employment level of GDP. Long run equilibrium can occur only at full employment.

- Congress can conduct **discretionary fiscal policy**. This includes government action on spending and taxes. In periods of high inflation, economic theory says taxes should be increased and government spending should be decreased. **Automatic stabilizers** can adjust the economy in these situations as well, without new action from Congress, through things like unemployment, progressive taxation, and transfer payments.

- Tax revenues decrease automatically as GDP falls, preventing consumption and the economy from falling further.

- Tax revenues increase automatically as GDP rises, slowing consumption and preventing the economy from overheating.

# An Introduction to Aggregate Demand

Student Alert: Make sure that when you label an AD/AS graph you use price level (PL) and real GDP (Y). Don't use P and Q – those are MICRO labels!

1.  Draw and properly label an Aggregate Demand curve that shows a shift of the curve left and a shift right.

2.  Explain how each of the following effects leads to an increase in real GDP when the price level falls.

    (A)  Interest rate effect

    (B)  Real wealth effect (or real balance effect)

    (C)  Exchange rate effect (or net export effect)

3.  Determine whether each change listed in Table 3-1.1 will cause an increase, decrease, or no change in AD. In column 1, list which component of AD is affected: C, I, G, or Xn. In column 2, write whether AD will increase or decrease. In column 3, write if the change from column two results in a leftward or rightward shift of the AD curve. In column 4, draw and label the AD curve, showing the correct shift.

*Table 3-1.1*
### CHANGES IN AGGREGATE DEMAND

| Change | 1. Component of AD | 2. Increase or Decrease? | 3. Shift left or right? | 4. Draw and label the shift in the AD graph |
|---|---|---|---|---|
| A  New tariffs on imported goods lead to a trade war that reduces exports by more than it reduces imports. | | | | |
| B  Reduced business confidence leads to a reduction in investment spending. | | | | |
| C  Government spending increases with no increase in taxes. | | | | |
| D  Survey shows consumer confidence jumps. | | | | |
| E  Reports of an impending recession create fear among households | | | | |
| F  The Federal Government eliminates the Department of Education. | | | | |

# Investment Demand

Investment spending consists of spending on new buildings, machinery, factories, and equipment. Investment spending is a part of aggregate expenditures in the economy. Any increase in investment spending will increase aggregate expenditures (GDP), thus increasing AD.

Decisions about investment spending are based on a comparison of marginal cost and marginal benefit. If a firm expects a particular project to yield a greater benefit than cost, it will undertake it. An important cost associated with investment spending is the interest expense. Firms must either borrow money to engage in an investment project or use their own money. In either case, the interest rate determines the cost of the investment project. If the firm borrows money to invest, it must pay the interest rate to borrow. If the firm uses its own money, then it gives up the interest it could have earned by loaning that money to someone else. That is, the interest rate measures the opportunity cost if a firm invests with its own money.

1.  Draw a graph illustrating an investment demand curve. Remember, the price paid to invest is the interest rate, so your graph should show the interest rate on the vertical axis, and the demand curve should have a slope that illustrates the relationship between the interest rate and the amount of investment a firm will undertake. Show on your graph how an interest rate increase from r to $r_1$ results in an investment decrease from I to $I_1$.

2.  What factors could cause a firm to invest more or less at any given level of the interest rate? That is, what could cause the investment demand curve to shift (increase or decrease)?

 AP Macroeconomics Student Workbook © Council for Economic Education, New York, NY

# UNIT 3 **ACTIVITY 3-2.1**

# Spending in the Economy

## PART A: MPC and MPS

1.  Fill in the blanks in Table 3-2.1.

 *Table 3-2.1*
**MARGINAL PROPENSITIES TO CONSUME AND TO SAVE**

| Disposable income | Consumption | Saving | MPC | MPS |
| --- | --- | --- | --- | --- |
| $12,000 | $12,100 | –$100 | — | — |
| $13,000 | $13,000 | $0 | 0.90 | 0.10 |
| $14,000 | $13,800 | $200 | | |
| $15,000 | $14,500 | $500 | | |
| $16,000 | $15,100 | $900 | | |
| $17,000 | $15,600 | $1,400 | | |

2.  Explain why the sum of MPC and MPS must always equal 1.

3.  You're headed to your favorite local store. In the parking lot, you look down and see a $100 bill. Based on what you buy in the store, what is your MPC? What is your MPS?

4.  How can saving be negative?

## PART B: The Spending Multiplier

The people in Econoland live on an isolated island. One year a stranger arrives and builds a factory to make seashell charms. The factory is considered an investment in Econoland. If the MPC on the island is 75 percent, or 0.75, it means that Econoland residents consume 75 percent of any change in income and save 25 percent of any change in income. The additional spending generates additional income and eventually a multiple increase in income.

This is called the multiplier effect. When they hear about the multiplier effect, the islanders are thrilled about the new factory because they like the idea of additional income. The residents of Econoland want to know what would eventually happen to the levels of GDP, consumption, and saving on the island as the new spending works its way through the economy. Luckily there is a retired economist on Econoland who offers a brief statement of the multiplier. "It's simple," he says, "One person's spending becomes another person's income." The economist gives a numerical example, as shown in Table 3-2.2. "This shows the process," he says. The rounds refer to the movement of spending from resident to resident.

*Table 3-2.2*

**CHANGES IN ECONOLAND'S GDP, CONSUMPTION, AND SAVING**

| Round | Income (GDP) | Consumption spending | Saving |
|---|---|---|---|
| Round 1 | $1,000 | 0.75 of $1,000 = $750.00 | 0.25 of $1,000 = $250.00 |
| Round 2 | One person's spending becoming another person's income: $750.00 | 0.75 of $750 = | 0.25 of $750 = |
| Round 3 | The next person's spending becoming another person's income: | 0.75 of = | 0.25 of = |
| Round 4 | The next person's spending becoming another person's income: | 0.75 of = | 0.25 of = |
| Rounds continue | ⋮ | ⋮ | ⋮ |
| All rounds | Final outcome for income (GDP)? | Final outcome for consumption spending? | Final outcome for saving? |

1. Fill in Table 3-2.2 to help the economist explain the multiplier effect to the citizens of Econoland.

   The retired economist summarizes the multiplier effect for the crowd of Econolanders. "This shows us that the factory is an investment that has a multiplied effect on our GDP. In this case, the multiplier is 4." He adds, "It appears to be magic, but it is simply that one person's spending becomes another person's income."

   To check for understanding, the old professor asks the citizens a series of questions. How would Econolanders answer these questions?

2. Would the multiplier be larger or smaller if you saved more of your additional income?

3. What do you think would happen if all Econolanders saved all of the change in their incomes?

4. If the MPC in Econoland was .5, what is the Multiplier? How much income would be created? Show your work.

5. If the MPS in Econoland was .10, what is the Multiplier? How much income would be created? Show your work.

# Calculating Multipliers

## The Spending Multiplier and the Tax Multiplier

**Multiplier Formulas and Terms**

MPC = ΔC/ΔDI     MPS = ΔS/ΔDI

**Spending Multiplier = 1/(1-MPC) or 1/MPS**

**Tax Multiplier = -MPC/(1-MPC) or -MPC/MPS**

1.  What is the value of the tax multiplier if the MPC is 0.80? Show your work. ____

2.  What is the value of the spending multiplier if the MPC is 0.67? Show your work. ____

3.  What is the tax multiplier if the MPS is 0.25? Show your work. ____

4.  If the multiplier equals 4, then the MPS equals _____

5.  Suppose the MPC is .90 and government spending increases by $50 billion. All else equal, how much will GDP change?

6.  The MPS of Country A is higher than the MPS of Country B. Which country will have a larger multiplier? Explain.

7.  Imagine the United States' GDP is declining and the government decides to stimulate the economy with increased government spending. If the MPC is .8, and the government spends $100 billion, what will the total change in GDP be?

8.  A concerned citizen states that lowering taxes by $100 billion would increase GDP more than increasing government spending by the same amount. The MPC is .8. Is this true? Explain why. Show your work.

# Shifts in Short-Run Aggregate Supply

In column 1, list which component of AS is affected: input prices, government actions, or productivity or none if it does not affect AS. In column 2, write if AS will shift left, right or no change. In column 3 draw the AS graph and show the correct shift, if any.

*Table 3-4.1*
**CHANGES IN AGGREGATE SUPPLY**

| Change | 1. Determinant of AS | 2. Shift left or right or no change? | 3. Draw the graph showing the AS shift. |
|---|---|---|---|
| (A) Unions negotiate higher wages. | | | |
| (B) K12 education increases human capital. | | | |
| (C) Government spending increases. | | | |
| (D) Giant natural gas discovery decreases energy prices. | | | |
| (E) Computer technology brings new efficiency to industry. | | | |
| (F) Government imposes strict environmental regulations. | | | |
| (G) Prices rise but production costs stay the same. | | | |

# Short-Run Equilibrium Price Level and Output

## Summarizing Aggregate Demand and Aggregate Supply Shifts

For each of the graphs below, identify the starting equilibrium PL and Y. Then show the shift given for each graph and identify the new equilibrium PL and Y. Indicate the resulting change in price level, unemployment, and real GDP by circling the up arrow for an increase or the down arrow for a decrease.

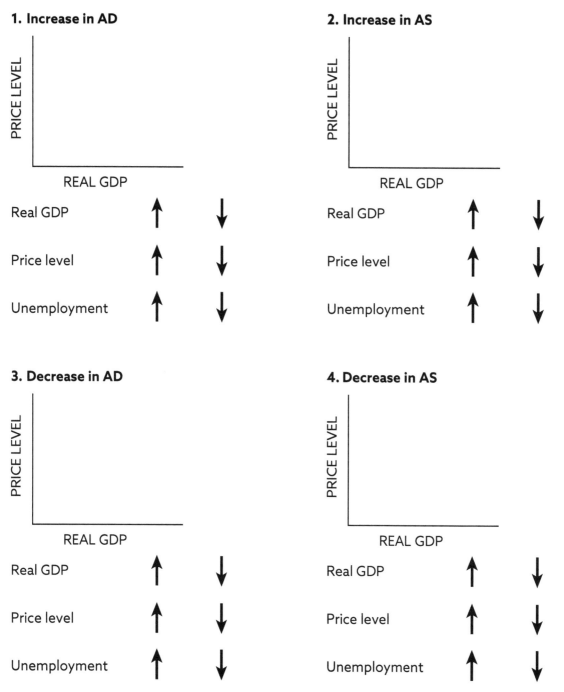

**1. Increase in AD**

PRICE LEVEL

REAL GDP

Real GDP ↑ ↓

Price level ↑ ↓

Unemployment ↑ ↓

**2. Increase in AS**

PRICE LEVEL

REAL GDP

Real GDP ↑ ↓

Price level ↑ ↓

Unemployment ↑ ↓

**3. Decrease in AD**

PRICE LEVEL

REAL GDP

Real GDP ↑ ↓

Price level ↑ ↓

Unemployment ↑ ↓

**4. Decrease in AS**

PRICE LEVEL

REAL GDP

Real GDP ↑ ↓

Price level ↑ ↓

Unemployment ↑ ↓

# Changes in Short-Run Aggregate Supply and Aggregate Demand

The equilibrium price and quantity in the economy will change when either the short-run aggregate supply (SRAS) or the aggregate demand (AD) curve shifts. The AD curve shifts when any of the components of AD change – consumption (C), investment (I), government spending (G), exports (X), or imports (M). The aggregate supply (AS) curve shifts when there are changes in the price of inputs (e.g., nominal wages, oil prices) or changes in productivity.

## Part A: Changes in the Equilibrium Price Level and Output

For each situation described below, illustrate the change on the AD and AS graph and describe the effect on the equilibrium price level and real gross domestic product (GDP) by circling the correct symbol: ↑ for increase, ↓ for decrease, or – for unchanged.

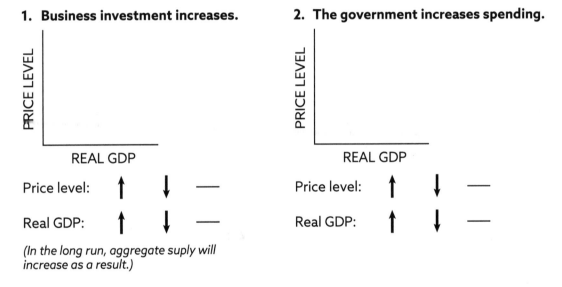

1. **Business investment increases.**

PRICE LEVEL

REAL GDP

Price level:   ↑   ↓   —

Real GDP:   ↑   ↓   —

*(In the long run, aggregate suply will increase as a result.)*

2. **The government increases spending.**

PRICE LEVEL

REAL GDP

Price level:   ↑   ↓   —

Real GDP:   ↑   ↓   —

**3. New oil discoveries cause large decreases in energy prices.**

Price level:  ↑   ↓   —

Real GDP:  ↑   ↓   —

**4. Consumer spending increases.**

Price level:  ↑   ↓   —

Real GDP:  ↑   ↓   —

**5. Production costs increase.**

Price level:  ↑   ↓   —

Real GDP:  ↑   ↓   —

**6. New technology and better education increase labor productivity.**

Price level:  ↑   ↓   —

Real GDP:  ↑   ↓   —

**7. Consumers' confidence improves.**

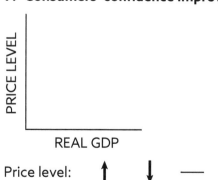

Price level:  ↑   ↓   —

Real GDP:  ↑   ↓   —

**8. Net exports decrease.**

Price level:  ↑   ↓   —

Real GDP:  ↑   ↓   —

## Part B: Graphing AD and AS

Draw an AD/AS graph to illustrate the change given in each of the questions below. On your graph be sure to label the axes (PL and Y), the AS and AD curves, and the starting and ending equilibrium PL and Y (these should be placed on the axes).

9.  Economic booms in both Japan and Europe result in massive increases in orders for exported goods from the United States.

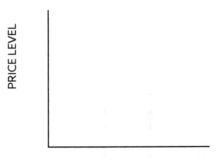

10. The government reduces taxes and increases transfer payments.

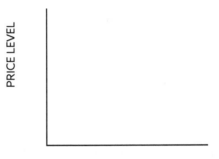

11. Fine weather results in the highest corn and wheat yields in 40 years.

12. While the United States was in the midst of the Great Depression, a foreign power attacked, Congress declared war, and more than 1,000,000 soldiers were drafted in the first year while defense spending was increased several times over.

13. To balance the budget, the federal government cuts Social Security payments by 10 percent and federal aid to education by 20 percent.

14. During a long, slow recovery from a recession, consumers postponed major purchases. Suddenly they begin to buy cars, refrigerators, televisions, and furnaces to replace their failing models.

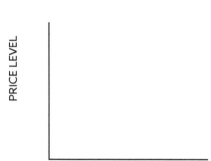

15. In response to other dramatic changes, the government raises taxes and reduces transfer payments in the hope of balancing the federal budget.

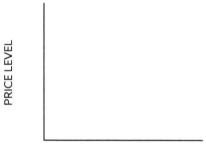

16. News of possible future layoffs frightens the public into reducing spending and increasing saving for the feared "rainy day."

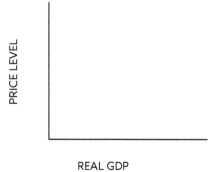

# UNIT 3 ACTIVITY 3-6.1

# Long-Run Aggregate Supply

In this activity we move from the short run to the long run. In the short run, at least one factor of production is fixed. In the long run, all factors of production are variable. The short-run aggregate supply (SRAS) curve is upward sloping because of slow wage and price adjustments in the economy.

But in the long run, wages and prices have time to adjust. That is, wages and prices are fully flexible. This means that any time the price level changes (i.e., there is inflation or deflation), wages and other input costs fully adjust so there is no overall effect. For example, if prices were doubled and wages and other input costs doubled, there would be no effect. Or if prices were cut in half, but so were wages and other input costs, there would be no effect. In the long run, wages and other input costs adjust so the economy always returns to the full-employment level of output. This means that the long-run aggregate supply (LRAS) curve is vertical at the full-employment output level (which is also called potential output).

Using Figure 3-6.1, answer the following questions about how the economy will react over time if the aggregate demand (AD) shifts from AD to $AD_1$.

Figure 3-6.1
**INCREASE IN AGGREGATE DEMAND STARTING AT FULL EMPLOYMENT**

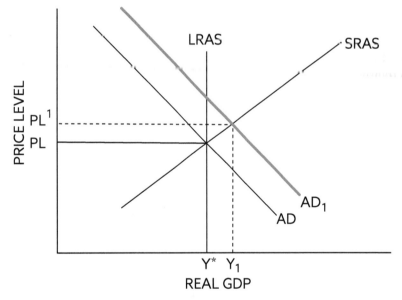

1. What will happen to output, nominal wages and real wages, and the price level in the short run? Explain.

2. What will happen to output and the price level when the economy moves to long-run equilibrium? How will workers and businesses react?

Using Figure 3-6.2, answer the following questions about how the economy will react and adjust over time if the aggregate supply (AS) shifts from SRAS to SRAS$_1$. Assume no government intervention.

*Figure 3-6.2*
**CHANGE IN SHORT-RUN AGGREGATE SUPPLY**

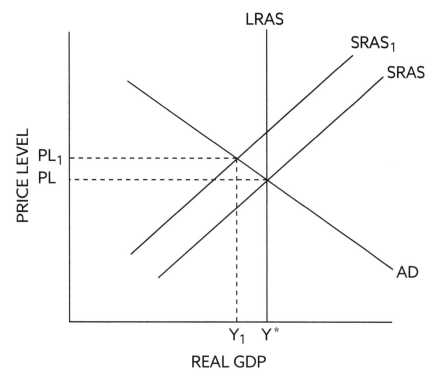

5.  After SRAS decreases, what happens to the short-run output, nominal wages, real wages, and the price level?

6.  What will happen to output and the price level when the economy moves to long-run equilibrium? Explain.

7.  On Figure 3-6.2, draw the long-run equilibrium situation (including PL, Y, and AS).

*Read the description of each change in AS or AD. Draw your own graph showing the starting point as long-run equilibrium, illustrated in Figure 3-6.3 below. Draw a new SRAS or AD curve that represents the change caused by the event described. Explain the reasons for the short-run change in the graph, and then explain what happens in the long run. Identify the final AD curve as ADf and the final SRAS curve as SRAS_f.*

Figure 3-6.3

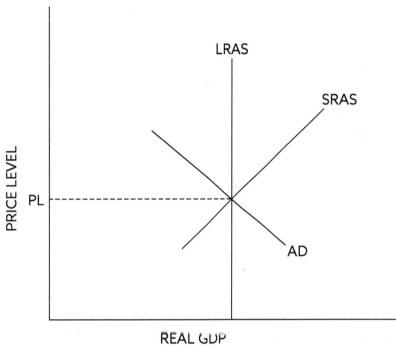

8. The government increases defense spending by 10 percent a year over a five-year period.

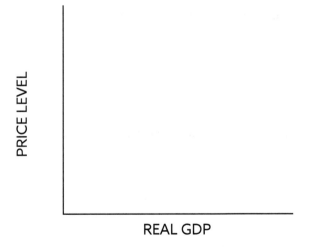

9. OPEC cuts oil production by 30 percent, and the world price of oil rises by 40 percent.

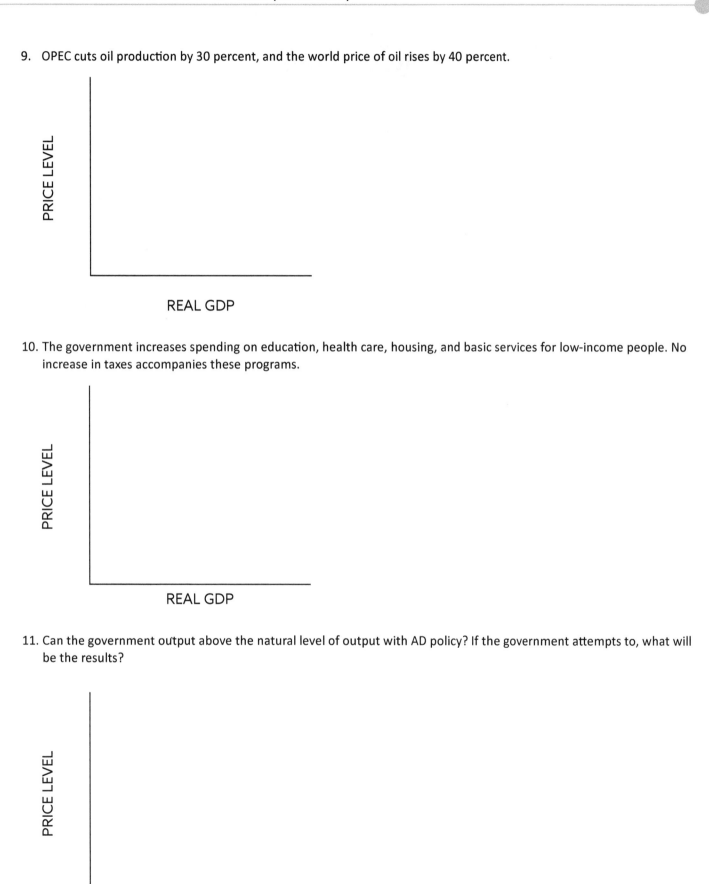

10. The government increases spending on education, health care, housing, and basic services for low-income people. No increase in taxes accompanies these programs.

11. Can the government output above the natural level of output with AD policy? If the government attempts to, what will be the results?

# Actual versus Full-Employment Output

The model of aggregate demand (AD) and aggregate supply (AS) predicts that the macroeconomy will come to equilibrium at the intersection of a downward-sloping AD curve and an upward sloping short-run aggregate supply (SRAS) curve. The short-run equilibrium is described as the only price level where the goods and services purchased by domestic and foreign buyers are equal to the quantity supplied within the economy. It's important to realize that, while the economy might be in equilibrium, this equilibrium level of output can be less than, equal to, or greater than full employment output.

Full-employment output is the level of real gross domestic product (GDP) that exists when the economy's unemployment rate is at its natural rate. This natural rate of unemployment doesn't correspond to an unemployment rate of zero; rather, it is the unemployment rate that exists when there is no cyclical unemployment. When the economy is recessionary, the unemployment rate will exceed this natural rate. When the economy is experiencing an inflationary gap, the unemployment rate will fall below the natural rate.

The distinction between the actual unemployment rate and the natural rate allows us to reconsider the short-run equilibrium in the macroeconomy. If AD and SRAS intersect at a level of output that falls below full-employment output (at the vertical long-run aggregate supply [LRAS] curve), the economy has a recessionary gap. If the AD and SRAS curves intersect at a real output that exceeds full employment, the economy has an inflationary gap.

1.  Draw an LRAS curve that illustrates a recessionary gap. Label the full-employment level of output on the graph.

2. Draw an LRAS curve that illustrates an inflationary gap. Label the full-employment level of output on the graph.

3. Suppose households in the United States experience a decrease in wealth. Assume the economy starts at long-run equilibrium as shown in Figure 3-6.4. Use the AS/AD model to show the short run effect on output, unemployment, and the price level.

*Figure 3-6.4*
**PRICE LEVEL**

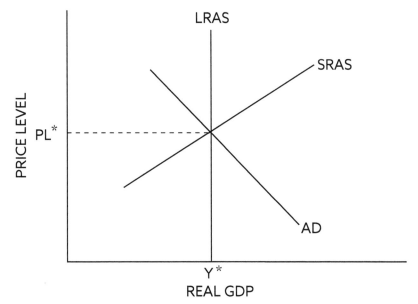

4. Will the unemployment rate increase or decrease? Explain.

5. What type of gap results from the decrease in wealth?

# The Types of Inflation

The aggregate supply (AS) and aggregate demand (AD) model is used to determine changes in the price level and real gross domestic product (GDP). Changes in AS and AD lead to changes in the price level (inflation and deflation). Whether changes in the price level are due to changes in AS or AD determines the type of inflation experienced in the economy. Demand-pull inflation is caused by a shift in the AD curve. Cost-push inflation is caused by a shift in the AS curve.

*Demand-pull inflation* occurs because the demand for goods and services increases at a time when the production of goods and services is already high. The increase in AD causes real GDP to expand and the price level to increase. Demand-pull inflation is often described by the saying "too much money chasing too few goods."

Figure 3-6.5 illustrates demand-pull inflation. An increase in AD causes the AD curve to shift to the right. AD will increase as a result of a change in the determinants of AD: consumption (C), investment (I), government spending (G), and net exports (Xn). Notice that, in addition to the increase in the price level, the increase in AD leads to an increase in real GDP.

*Figure 3-6.5*
**CHANGES IN THE PRICE LEVEL DUE TO AGGREGATE DEMAND**

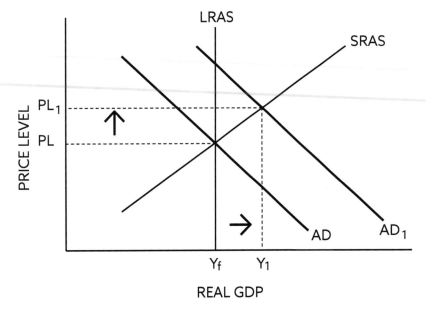

# UNIT 3 **ACTIVITY 3-6.3** (continued)

*Cost-push inflation* is caused by an increase in the cost of an input with economy-wide importance. An increase in production costs throughout the economy will cause AS to decrease. For example, an increase in wages or the price of oil will increase input costs economy-wide.

Figure 3-6.6 illustrates cost-push inflation. A decrease in AS causes the AS curve to shift to the left. AS will decrease as a result of an increase in production costs throughout the economy. Notice that, in addition to the increase in the price level, the decrease in AS leads to a decrease in real GDP. *Stagflation* occurs when the economy experiences high inflation and high unemployment at the same time.

*Figure 3-6.6*
**CHANGES IN THE PRICE LEVEL DUE TO AGGREGATE SUPPLY**

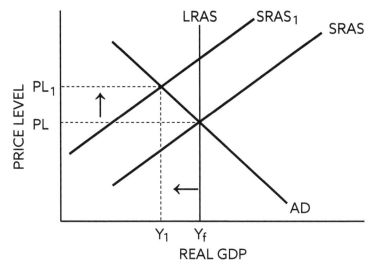

For each situation described below, CIRCLE either demand-pull or cost-push inflation and explain.

1.  In her 2028 State of the Union address, President Dodge calls for an increase in the U.S. military presence across the globe to combat what she deemed a "threat to the sovereignty of the U.S. economy and trade routes."

    Demand-Pull Inflation or Cost-Push Inflation

    Explain:

2.  The global pandemic of 2020 disrupts production and labor force availability worldwide.

    Demand-Pull Inflation or Cost-Push Inflation

    Explain:

3.  Congress and the president pass and sign legislation providing Medicare for all Americans. As a result of the expansion of healthcare, the government runs a budget deficit with increased government borrowing.

    Demand-Pull Inflation or Cost-Push Inflation

    Explain:

4.  In the 1970's the price of oil was controlled by OPEC, who raised prices and increased costs in all sectors of the economy that relied on oil.

    Demand-Pull Inflation or Cost-Push Inflation

    Explain:

# The Tools of Fiscal Policy

## Part A

Changes in taxes and government spending designed to affect the level of aggregate demand in the economy are called fiscal policy.

For Questions 1 – 4, decide whether each of the following fiscal policies of the federal government is expansionary or contractionary. Write expansionary or contractionary and EXPLAIN the reasons for your choice.

1. The government cuts business and personal income taxes and increases its own spending.

2. The government increases the personal income tax, Social Security tax, and corporate tax. Government spending stays the same.

3. Government spending goes up while taxes remain the same.

4. The government reduces the wages of its employees while raising taxes on consumers and businesses. Other government spending remains the same.

For Questions 5 – 6, use the Multiplier to determine the answer.

5. The economy is too hot and Congress wants to prevent inflation from rising so they vote to raise taxes by $200b. Assume that Americans save 20% of the change in their disposable income. Calculate the effect of these taxes on the U.S. economy.

6. The people who live in the country of Econoland spend 3/4ths of their disposable income. The Econoland government increased its spending by $50 trillion to stimulate the economy but are also worried about increasing the national debt so they also increased taxes by $50 trillion. Calculate the effect of these changes on the Econoland Aggregate Demand.

## Part B

Test your understanding of fiscal policy by completing Table 3-7.1. For each of the scenarios, identify if expansionary or contractionary policy is needed. Next, identify if that fiscal policy requires either an increase or decrease in both taxation and government spending. (Hint: Fiscal policy cannot provide a solution to one of these situations.) Fill in the spaces as follows:

*Table 3-7.1*
**EFFECTS OF FISCAL POLICY**

|  | (A) Expansionary or Contractionary? | (B) Taxation: Increase or Decrease? | (C) Spending: Increase or Decrease? |
|---|---|---|---|
| 1. National unemployment rate rises to 12 percent. |  |  |  |
| 2. Inflation is strong at a rate of 14% per year. |  |  |  |
| 3. The economy is experiencing stagflation. Inflation is increasing rapidly and unemployment is high. |  |  |  |
| 4. Business sales and investment are expanding rapidly, and economists think strong inflation lies ahead. |  |  |  |
| 5. Surveys show consumers are losing confidence in the economy, retail sales are weak, and business inventories are increasing rapidly. |  |  |  |

# Discretionary Fiscal Policy and Automatic Stabilizers

For each of the scenarios on the following page, indicate whether it represents an automatic (A) or discretionary (D) stabilizer, and whether it is an example of expansionary (E) or contractionary (C) fiscal policy.

*Table 3-8.1*
**ECONOMIC SCENARIOS**

| Economic Scenarios | Automatic (A) or Discretionary (D) | Expansionary (E) or Contractionary (C) |
|---|---|---|
| Recession raises amount of unemployment compensation. | | |
| The government cuts personal income tax rates. | | |
| The government eliminates favorable tax treatment on long-term capital gains. | | |
| Incomes rise; as a result, people pay a larger fraction of their income in taxes. | | |
| As a result of a recession, more families qualify for food stamps and welfare benefits. | | |
| The government eliminates the interest expense deduction for tax purposes. | | |
| The government launches a major new space program to explore Mars. | | |
| The government raises Social Security taxes on paychecks. | | |
| Corporate profits increase; as a result, government collects more corporate income taxes. | | |
| The government raises corporate income tax rates. | | |
| The government gives all its employees a large pay raise. | | |

# Automatic Stabilizers Effect on AD/AS

When there are output gaps (inflationary or recessionary) Congress can enact fiscal policy. Because this takes time, however, the first line of defense against output gaps are automatic stabilizers.

For each of the following graphs, explain what type of automatic stabilizer would help bring the economy back to full employment output. Note that the equilibrium point referenced on the graph at Y and PLe is the original equilibrium before the curve shifted.

 *Figure 3-8.1*

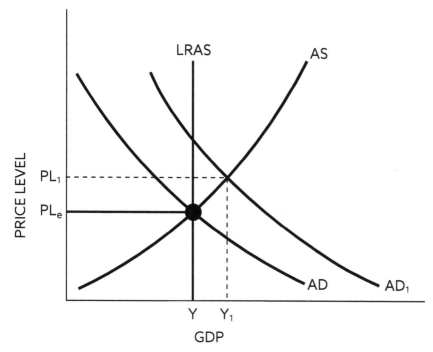

1. What type of gap is seen in the economy above? _____

2. Name an automatic stabilizer that would bring the above economy to full employment.

3. If the economy did not return back to full employment, should Congress implement contractionary or expansionary fiscal policy? _____

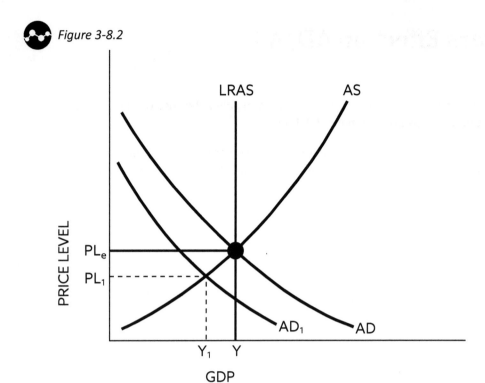

Figure 3-8.2

1.  What type of gap is seen in the economy above? _____

2.  Name an automatic stabilizer that would bring the above economy to full employment.



3.  If the economy did not return back to full employment, should Congress implement contractionary or expansionary fiscal policy? _____

# UNIT 4
## THE FINANCIAL SECTOR

# UNIT 4 **MACROECONOMICS KEY IDEAS**

- Money can take many forms and is defined as anything that serves the three main functions of money: a medium of exchange, a unit of account, and a store of value.

- Financial assets include stocks and bonds. They represent a claim that entitles the buyer to future income from the seller.

- The most liquid forms of money are cash and demand deposits.

- The opportunity cost of holding money is the interest that could have been earned from holding other financial assets such as bonds.

- The money supply is measured by monetary aggregates M1 and M2. M1 includes liquid assets and M2 is a broader definition of the money supply and consists of M1 plus less liquid assets.

- In a fractional reserve banking system, demand deposits lead to money creation. Money is created through the money multiplier process when banks make loans, and it is destroyed when loans are repaid.

- After the 2008 Financial Crisis, in order to fix the problem, the Federal Reserve changed the American banking system to an ample reserve system, where bank reserves are now in the trillions and banks have additional deposits at the Fed that can earn interest (interest on reserve balance (IORB) rate).

- Banks were required under a limited reserve system to keep a percentage of their deposits as reserves. Reserves can be currency in the bank vault or deposits at the Federal Reserve Banks. The reserve requirement limits the amount of money banks can create. Due to the change to the ample reserve system and the liquidity and emergency loans needed during the Pandemic, the Federal Reserve no longer requires banks to hold excess reserves, but the reserve requirement rate and the deposit expansion multiplier are still important AP Test concepts.

- The simple deposit expansion multiplier is equal to 1 divided by the required reserve ratio (rr). Deposit expansion multiplier = 1 / rr

- The amount predicted by the simple money multiplier may be overstated because it does not take into account a bank's desire to hold excess reserves or the public holding more currency.

- The demand for money is the sum of transactions demand, precautionary demand, and speculative demand. The demand for money is determined by interest rates, income, and the price level. The supply of money is set by the Federal Reserve (the Fed). Equilibrium in the money market determines the interest rate in the economy.

- The loanable funds market is made up of lenders, who supply funds, and borrowers, who demand funds. Equilibrium in the loanable funds market determines the interest rate and quantity of loanable funds.

- The Federal Reserve regulates financial institutions and controls the nation's money supply.

- The federal funds rate (FFR) is the interest rate a bank charges when it lends excess reserves to other banks. The Fed currently targets the FFR to implement monetary policy because it is closely tied to economic activity.

- A nominal interest rate is the rate of interest paid for a loan, unadjusted for inflation. Lenders and borrowers establish nominal interest rates as the sum of their expected real interest rate and expected inflation.

- The Federal Reserve regulates financial institutions and controls the nation's money supply. In the previous limited reserves system, the three main tools that the Fed can use to control the money supply are buying and selling government bonds (open market operations), changing the discount rate, and changing the reserve requirement. In the new ample reserves system, the old powers are not effective at changing the federal funds rate because reserves are too ample to make a difference. The new main power is adjusting the administered rates, most notably the interest on reserve balance (IORB) rate, which is the rate that banks earn on keeping deposits at the Federal Reserve.

- Under a limited reserve system, if a central bank wants to increase the money supply, it will encourage bank lending by buying bonds, decreasing the discount rate, or decreasing the reserve requirement. This is referred to as expansionary monetary policy and is used by the Fed to reduce unemployment and increase aggregate demand.

- Under an ample reserve system, if the Fed wants to increase the money supply, it will lower the IORB – interest on reserve balance rate (the base rate of profit for the banks) which will cause banks to lower the federal funds rate to each other, and then the nominal rate to the public.

- Under a limited reserve system, if a central bank wants to decrease the money supply, it will discourage bank lending by selling bonds, increasing the discount rate, or increasing the reserve requirement. This is called contractionary monetary policy and is used to control inflation.

- Under an ample reserve system, the Fed will raise the IORB – interest on reserve balance rate (administered rate). This will increase the floor profit of banks if they just leave reserves at the federal reserve. This will cause banks to raise the Federal Funds rate to each other, since there is more incentive to lend at a higher rate than the base profit they are getting at the Federal Reserve. This will cause banks to then raise the nominal interest rate to the public.

- Open market operations are the most frequently used tool in the limited reserve system, but they are only used to maintain ample reserves in the ample reserve system.

- Long term interest rates also have long term effects on long-run aggregate supply curve (LRAS) Since investment spending is very interest sensitive, it will cause either a long-term increase or decrease in the capital stock, which will either increase or decrease LRAS.

- In reality, there are lags to monetary policy caused by the time it takes to recognize a problem in the economy and the time it takes the economy to adjust to the policy action.

# Introduction to Financial Assets

---

Student Alert: Table 4-1.1 shows finanical assets in order from least risky to most risky. Demand deposits secured by the FDIC are the least risky. Individual stocks are the riskiest assets in this chart.  !

---

*Table 4-1.1*
**FINANCIAL ASSETS OVERVIEW**

| Asset | Description | Potential Growth Rate |
|---|---|---|
| **Checking Account** | • A basic demand deposit, which is a bank account from which deposited funds can be withdrawn at any time, without advance notice.<br><br>• Very liquid store of value (an asset that can easily be converted into cash in a short amount of time) and easy to go from store of value to medium of exchange; as you can use your debit card, electronic pay, or ATM to access your money.<br><br>• Most balances are fully insured by the Federal Deposit Insurance Corporation (FDIC). | • Very low or no interest since this is a very liquid account, and the value is constantly changing. |
| **Savings Account** | • Bank accounts that are less liquid than checking. Meant to be used primarily as a store of value with the potential to transfer money electronically from your checking into your savings (and vice versa)<br><br>• Insured by the Federal Deposit Insurance Corporation (FDIC). Cannot decrease in value unless you transfer money/withdraw from it. | • Very low interest rate. Does not decrease in value unless you withdraw. Higher yield savings accounts do exist but are rare. |

---

*Table 4-1.1*

**FINANCIAL ASSETS OVERVIEW (CONTINUED)**

| Asset | Description | Potential Growth Rate |
|---|---|---|
| **Certificate of Deposit (time deposit)** | • A certificate of deposit is a type of bank savings product that earns interest on a lump sum for a fixed period of time. However, that lump sum must remain untouched for the period of time or face withdrawal penalties.<br><br>• Insured by the Federal Deposit Insurance Corporation (FDIC). Cannot decrease in value. | • Higher interest than other accounts as a reward for the decrease in liquidity. |
| **Money Market Account** | • This is a deposit account in which the bank invests the owner's money in regulated funds but the bank, not the owner, takes the risk. Since the bank is using this money to invest, account owner withdrawals are limited.<br><br>• Insured by the Federal Deposit Insurance Corporation (FDIC). Cannot decrease in value. | • Earns interest that is generally higher than a standard bank account as a reward for the decrease in liquidity. |
| **Money Market Fund** | • An investment that earns interest and income at a rate determined by the interest rates of the underlying assets in the fund. With this type of account, the owner is investing money in the market—the money can decrease in value based upon market conditions.<br><br>• This is considered low risk but is uninsured and can decrease in value. | • Rates are typically higher, and there is the ability to earn passive income on top of the value. |

*Table 4-1.1*
**FINANCIAL ASSETS OVERVIEW (CONTINUED)**

| Asset | Description | Potential Growth Rate |
|-------|-------------|----------------------|
| **Bonds** | • Bonds are a financial asset that are a loan to the government or corporation. Bonds are IOUs and people give these entities loans and are paid back after a certain period of time, called a maturity date with the principal (initial amount) plus a yearly compounded fixed interest rate. Some bonds offer a coupon rate in which the fixed interest rate acts as a percent of yearly income of the lump value.<br><br>• Bonds cannot decrease in value, but the bond issuer can default if they do not have the funds or go bankrupt.<br><br>• The bond's value remains fixed for the life of the bond. However, new bonds will be based on new national nominal interest rates. If the nominal interest rate increases, new bonds will be issued at this higher rate. If people with the original bond want to sell their bonds before they mature, they have to offer a discounted price because other investors would rather just buy the higher yield bonds. The price of previously issued bonds and interest rates on bonds are inversely related. | • A higher rate than savings accounts and a wide variety of bonds from Municipalities to the Treasury Department. Government bonds have a lower interest rate because they are lower risk. Corporate Bonds also have a higher interest rate based on the higher risk of defaulting.<br><br>• Bonds are a "safer" investment than stocks because they have a guaranteed profit and do not fluctuate in their nominal value. There are different levels of Bonds rated from AAA-down; with the higher the risk reflecting a higher interest rate and shorter maturity date, and the lower risk reflecting longer maturity date and lower interest rate. |
| **Stocks** | • Stocks are actual ownership of a share of a company. The value of the stock is based on the demand that people are willing to pay to own a piece of the company, its success, stability, and outlook.<br><br>• People who own shares of stock can make money by holding onto a stock and hoping the value of it increases and then selling it. Stocks change value by people's confidence and fear in the company, industry, and economy.<br><br>• Some stocks also offer dividends; passive income as a percentage of the stock price. Since shareholders are also "owners" of the company, some Board of Directors issue dividends per share of stock people own. | • Stocks technically have an unlimited ceiling based on how companies perform, their history, outlook, and how much people are willing to pay to own a "share" of that company.<br><br>• Dividends have the potential to create passive income and dividend reinvestment plans (DRIPS) allow for using your dividends to purchase more shares of the stock; increasing the size of your portfolio.<br><br>• However, stocks also are based on their companies, so if a company goes bankrupt then the stock becomes worthless. |

1. Although being conservative with money may be advantageous, why would you NOT want to be too conservative?

2. For different types of bank accounts, why is interest a reward for less liquidity?

3. Why can it be said that bonds preserve wealth but stocks grow wealth?

4. For each scenario, what asset(s) would you recommend the person potentially put their money in?

   (A) Bryanna is 18 years old and received $1,000 in graduation gifts. Explain.

   (B) Kristine is 23 and has an extra $300 a month after bills. Explain.

   (C) Hamza has saved $5,000 working part time and he needs to pay for college in the next 6 months. Explain.

   (D) It is a recession. Leah has $2,000 saved. Would you recommend her to be aggressive with the money or wait until the economy improves? Explain.

   (E) Noah is a high school student, just got his first paycheck of $400 for part time work and is going to his local bank for a place to put his money. What introductory bank account(s) would you advise him to open up? Explain.

   (F) Ryan has $3,000 saved in his savings account and is looking to be slightly more aggressive with his money but does not want to invest in individual stocks himself. Would you recommend a money market account, money market fund or bonds? Explain.

   (G) Thomas has $10,000 saved and wants to buy a home in about 5 years. Your advice? Explain why.

   (H) You inherited $20,000 from your great-aunt. Your MPC is .50. How much are you investing and where would YOU invest this money? Why?

# UNIT 4 **ACTIVITY 4-2.1**

# The Time Value of Money

## Calculating Real and Nominal Interest Rates

### Part A: Real vs. Nominal

1.  The inflation rate is 3%, and you have a yearly dividend on a stock that is 5%, how much is your investment growing by, when adjusted for inflation? _____

2.  You have a bond that has a yearly interest rate of 4% but the inflation rate is 2%.What is the real interest rate your bond earned this year? _____

3.  If a bank wants to maintain a real profit of 2%, but inflation is expected to be 5%, what is the nominal interest rate that they will charge customers? _____

4.  If banks expect inflation to be 3% and they want to maintain a real profit of 3% what is the nominal interest rate that they charge customers? _____

5.  You just got a 5% raise, but inflation is expected to be 7%. In real terms, did you get more money in your paycheck? Explain.

6.  Why would people who borrow at fixed rate loans (the nominal interest rate remains the same for the life of the loan) "benefit" from unexpected inflation.

7.  Why would people who have fixed incomes and retirement savings be hurt during unexpected periods of inflation?

### Part B: The Rule of 72

8.  Doug invested $2,500 into a Certificate of Deposit earning a 6.5% interest rate. Approximately how many years will it take Doug's investment to double?

9.  Emily has a $2,200 balance on her credit card with an 18% interest rate. If she chooses to not make any payments and does not receive late charges, approximately how many years will it take for her balance to double?

10. Approximately how many years will it take your money to double?

    (A) 2% interest _____

    (B) 6% interest _____

    (C) 12% interest _____

AP Macroeconomics Student Workbook © Council for Economic Education, New York, NY

103

# Understanding Money – Its Categories and Functions

## Questions:

1. What do the categories of M1 and M2 tell us about the different ways money can be stored? What conclusions about our financial system and banking system can you draw just based on this list?

2. Why is it a good personal finance practice to have a variety of different types of M1 and M2 accounts?

3. What is the difference between liquid and non-liquid?

4. M2 accounts typically have higher interest rates as a reward for being less liquid. Why might banks want your deposits to be less liquid?

5. Savings Accounts and Money Market accounts used to be M2. How might have technology made them more liquid where they are now counted as M1?

6. Why would retirement accounts not be included in M1 or M2?

7. Why would the Federal Reserve make the formula for categorizing money as M2 = M1 +M2?

Extra Credit: Research your local bank. What financial accounts do they offer?

# Money Classifications and Calculations

In each of the following scenarios, which function of money is being served? Indicate M for medium of exchange, S for store of value, or U for unit of account.

\_\_\_\_ 1. You pay for your lunch with a $20 bill.

\_\_\_\_ 2. A car is described as being worth $18,000.

\_\_\_\_ 3. A grandparent puts $500 into a savings account for a grandchild's future.

\_\_\_\_ 4. You decide you want to give $10 worth of candy to a friend for his birthday.

\_\_\_\_ 5. A driver pays a $5 toll.

\_\_\_\_ 6. You set aside $10 per week to save up for a new computer.

8. Why are credit cards not considered money? Do they serve any of the functions of money?


9. Order the list of assets below from 1 to 5, with 1 being most liquid and 5 being least liquid.

\_\_\_\_ a $10 bill

\_\_\_\_ a traveler's check

\_\_\_\_ a certificate of deposit

\_\_\_\_ a savings account deposit share

\_\_\_\_ a retirement account

*Table 4-3.2*
**CALCULATING THE MONEY SUPPLY**

|  | In billions of dollars |
| --- | --- |
| Checkable deposits (demand deposits, NOW, ATM, and credit union share draft accounts) | $1,500 |
| Currency in circulation | $1,000 |
| Savings deposits | $7,000 |
| Small-denomination time deposits | $500 |
| Credit card balances | $2,000 |
| Money market funds | $600 |

10. Use the data in Table 4-3.2 to calculate M1 and M2 in billions of dollars. Assume all items not mentioned are zero.

(A) M1 = _____

(B) M2 = _____

# UNIT 4 **ACTIVITY 4-4.1**

# Banks and the Creation of Money

To see how a bank can create money and expand the money supply in the economy, consider the following scenario.

1.  A new checkable deposit of $1,000 is made in Bank 1. The required reserve ratio is 10 percent of checkable deposits, and banks do not hold any excess reserves. That is, banks loan out the other 90 percent of their deposits. Assume that all money loaned out by one bank is redeposited in another bank. To see how the new deposit creates money and increases the money supply, find the following values.

    (A)  Bank 1 must keep required reserves = _____

    (B)  Bank 1 can loan = _____

    (C)  When the proceeds of the loan are redeposited, Bank 2 receives new deposits = _____

    (D)  Bank 2 must keep additional required reserves = _____

    (E)  Bank 2 can now make new loans = _____

    (F)  When the proceeds of the loan are redeposited, Bank 3 receives new deposits = _____

    (G)  Bank 3 must keep additional required reserves = _____

    (H)  Bank 3 can now make new loans = _____

2.  Use your answers from above to complete Table 4-4.1. Round the values to two decimals (e.g., $59.05). After you have completed the table, fill in the blanks in the statements that follow.

Table 4-4.1
CHECKABLE DEPOSITS, RESERVES, AND LOANS IN SEVEN BANKS

| Bank | New checkable deposits | 10% required reserves | Loans |
|---|---|---|---|
| 1 | $1,000.00 | $100.00 | $900.00 |
| 2 | | | |
| 3 | | | |
| 4 | | | $656.10 |
| 5 | | | |
| 6 | $590.49 | $59.05 | |
| 7 | $531.44 | | $478.30 |
| All other banks combined | | | |
| Total for all banks | $10,000.00 | | $9,000.00 |

(A) The original deposit of $1,000 increased total bank reserves by _____. Eventually, this led to a total of $10,000 expansion of bank deposits, _____ of which was because of the original deposit, while _____ was because of bank lending activities.

(B) If the required reserve had been 15 percent instead of 10 percent, the amount of deposit expansion would have been (more/less) than in this example.

(C) If the fractional reserve had been 5 percent instead of 10 percent, the amount of deposit expansion would have been (more/less) than in this example.

(D) If banks had not loaned out all of their excess reserves, the amount of deposit expansion would have been (more/less) than in this example.

(E) If all loans had not been redeposited in the banking system, the amount of deposit expansion would have been (more/less) than in this example.

3.  Another way to represent the multiple expansion of deposits is through a *T-account* or Balance Sheet. A T-account shows offsetting assets and liabilities. For the bank, assets include loans, deposits with the Federal Reserve, and Treasury securities. Liabilities include deposits. Use the T-account below to show how the new $1,000 deposit described in the previous example would be listed in a T-account.

*Table 4-4.2*
**T-ACCOUNT**

| Assets | Liabilities |
|---|---|
|  |  |

> Student Alert: Make sure you read any money multiplier questions carefully to determine exactly which value the question asks for. For example, does it ask you to calculate the initial change or the final change? ⚠

4. Assume that $1,000 is deposited in the bank, and that each bank loans out all of its excess reserves. For each of the following required reserve ratios, calculate the amount that the bank must hold in required reserves, the amount that will be excess reserves, the deposit expansion multiplier, and the maximum amount that the money supply could increase.

*Table 4-4.3*
**REQUIRED RESERVE RATIOS**

|  | Required reserve ratio | | |
|---|---|---|---|
|  | 1% | 5% | 10% |
| Required reserves |  |  |  |
| Excess reserves |  |  |  |
| Deposit expansion multiplier |  |  |  |
| Maximum increase in the money supply |  |  |  |

(A) Will an increase in the reserve requirement increase or decrease the money supply? Explain.

(B) What will happen to deposits, required reserves, excess reserves, and the money supply if deposits are withdrawn from the banking system?

(C) What could happen at each stage of the money creation process to prevent the money supply from increasing to its full amount as determined by the deposit expansion multiplier?

(D) The Federal Reserve has eliminated all reserve requirements and banks now hold only excess reserves. What does it mean if the reserve requirement is 0? What does that do to the money multiplier?

# The Money Market

1.  Suppose there is an increase in the money supply. Draw a graph that shows an increase in the money supply and the resulting change in the equilibrium interest rate. What happened to the interest rate? What happens to the quantity of money demanded when the interest rate changes? Explain.

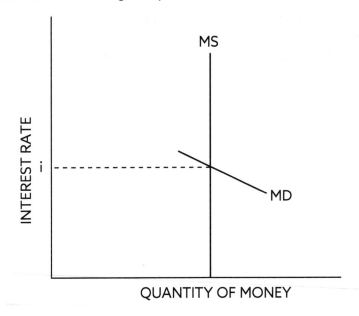

2. Draw a new graph of the money market, illustrating the equilibrium interest rate. Now imagine the economy is in a recession and unemployment is high. How will it affect the demand for money and the nominal interest rate? Illustrate the change on a money market graph. Explain how the types of demand shifted the graph in this example.

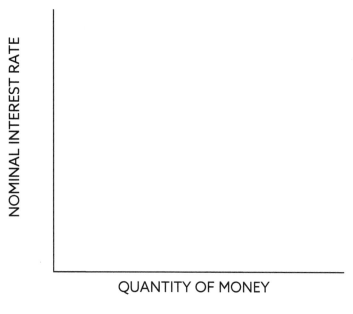

NOMINAL INTEREST RATE

QUANTITY OF MONEY

3. Draw a new graph of the money market, illustrating the equilibrium interest rate. Imagine that nominal GDP increases. Graph the changes. How will that affect the demand for money and the nominal interest rate?

INTEREST RATE

QUANTITY OF MONEY

# The Loanable Funds Market

The loanable funds market is made up of borrowers, who demand funds ($D_{lf}$), and depositors who supply funds ($S_{lf}$). The loanable funds market determines the real interest rate (the price of loans), as shown in Figure 4-6.1.

*Figure 4-6.1*
**MARKET FOR LOANABLE FUNDS**

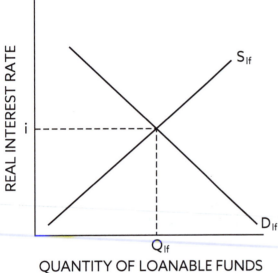

Student Alert: Make sure you understand the differences (and similarities) between the money market and the loanable funds market and use the appropriate one! The slope of the supply curve is a key distinction!

1. Why would the y-axis be the real and not the nominal interest rate? Explain.

2. Explain why the demand for loanable funds is negatively sloped. (Use the business borrower in your explanation.)

3. How are real interest rates to banks as prices are to businesses? How does this affect the slope of the supply curve?

4.  Why would the opportunity cost of not saving be higher as the real interest rate increases? How does this affect the slope of the supply curve?

5.  Draw a graph of the loanable funds market showing the effect of each of the following on the real interest rate and quantity of loanable funds. Draw the graph and explain why the curve shifts.

    (A)  The government increases spending without increasing taxes. Draw the graph and explain why the curve shifts.

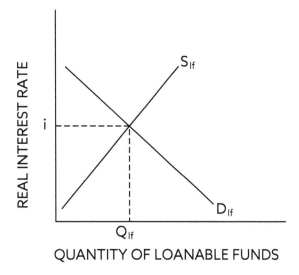

    (B)  The government increases the tax on income from interest payments. Draw the graph and explain why the curve shifts.

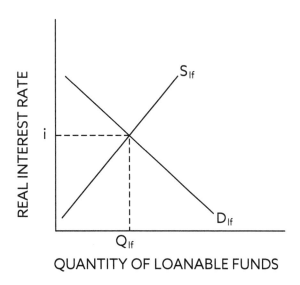

# UNIT 4 **ACTIVITY 4-6.1** (continued)

(C) The Federal Reserve buys bonds on the open market facilitating to help keep reserves ample amid a time of high withdrawals from the banking system. Draw the graph and explain why the curve shifts.

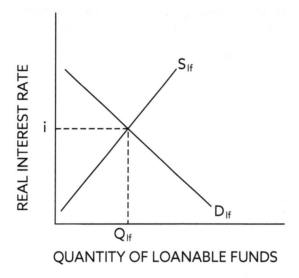

(D) The University of Michigan releases the index of consumer and business confidence, which indicates both are lower. Draw the graph and explain why the curve shifts.

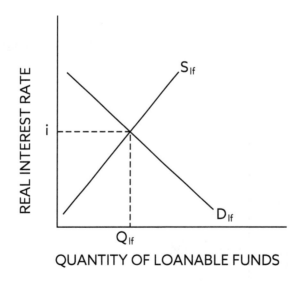

AP Macroeconomics Student Workbook © Council for Economic Education, New York, NY

(E) The Canadian banking system has a higher real interest rate compared to the American banking system. Draw the graph and explain why the curve shifts.

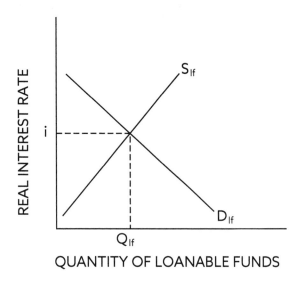

# An Overview of the Federal Reserve System

Following the widespread bank failures during the Panic of 1907 in the United States, industrialist and banker J.P. Morgan intervened to rescue the banking system by purchasing failing banks. Recognizing the need for stability and regulation in the banking sector, government officials and prominent figures within the banking industry collaborated to establish a new central bank. In 1913, the Federal Reserve Act was passed, leading to the creation of the Federal Reserve System. This marked the end of nearly eight decades without a central bank in the United States.

1.  Why was the Federal Reserve created?

2.  How is the Federal Reserve both a private and public institution? Do you think this is a good policy? Why or why not?

3.  Why would the institution be called "The Federal Reserve System?"

4.  Which of its financial roles do you think is the most important? Why?

5.  Which group makes decisions about monetary policy? How many members serve in this group? The president of which branch of the Fed is always a member? Why do you think that is?

6.  How do regional Federal Reserve Banks contribute to the functioning of the Federal Reserve System?

7.  What are three differences between the Federal Reserve and the European Central Bank?

# Fed Actions and Their Effects Graphic Organizer

> Student Alert: Open market operations include buying and selling government bonds. ⊙ When you are asked about an open market operation, you should answer in terms of buying bonds or selling bonds.

Complete Activity 4-8.1. Illustrate how the Fed's Monetary Policy creates a chain reaction throughout the banking system to increase or decrease AD.

## Fed Actions and Their Effects

| Type of Reserve | Federal Reserve Action | Bank Reserves | Money Supply | Federal Funds Rate | Nominal Interest Rate | Borrowing & Investment Spending | AD |
|---|---|---|---|---|---|---|---|
| Limited | Sold Treasury securities on the open market | | | | | | |
| Limited | Bought Treasury securities on the open market | | | | | | |
| Limited /Ample | Raises the discount rate | | | | | | |
| Limited /Ample | Lowered the discount rate | | | | | | |
| Limited | Lowered the reserve requirement | | | | | | |
| Limited | Raised the reserve requirement | | | | | | |
| Ample | Increase Interest on Reserve Balance Rate | | | | | | |
| Ample | Decrease Interest on Reserve Balance Rate | | | | | | |

# Market For Reserves: Limited System – Ample System

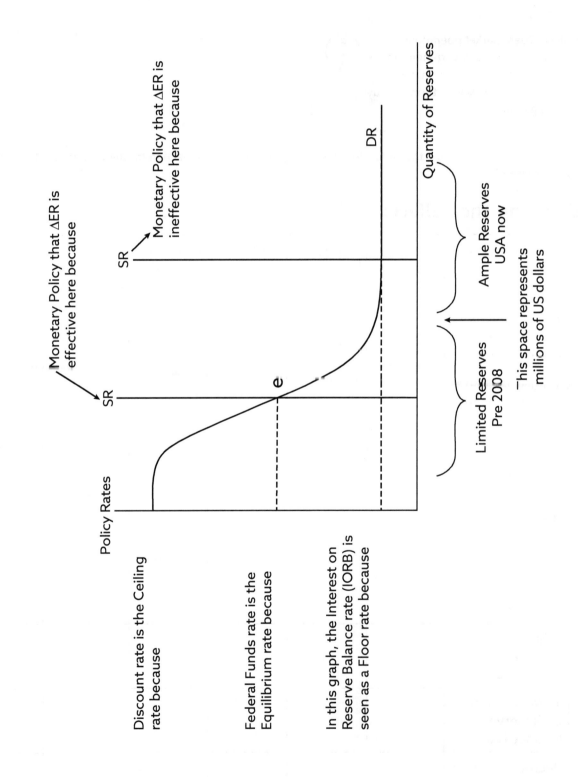

Policy Rates

Monetary Policy that ΔER is
effective here because

SR

Monetary Policy that ΔER is
ineffective here because

SR

e

DR

Limited Reserves
Pre 2008

Ample Reserves
USA now

This space represents
millions of US dollars

Quantity of Reserves

Discount rate is the Ceiling
rate because

Federal Funds rate is the
Equilibrium rate because

In this graph, the Interest on
Reserve Balance rate (IORB) is
seen as a Floor rate because

# Contractionary Monetary Policy

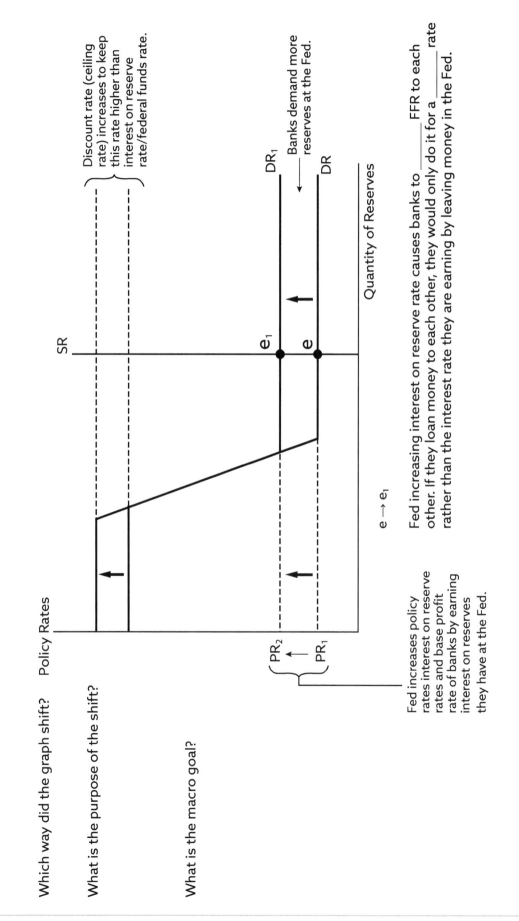

Which way did the graph shift?

What is the purpose of the shift?

What is the macro goal?

# Expansionary Monetary Policy

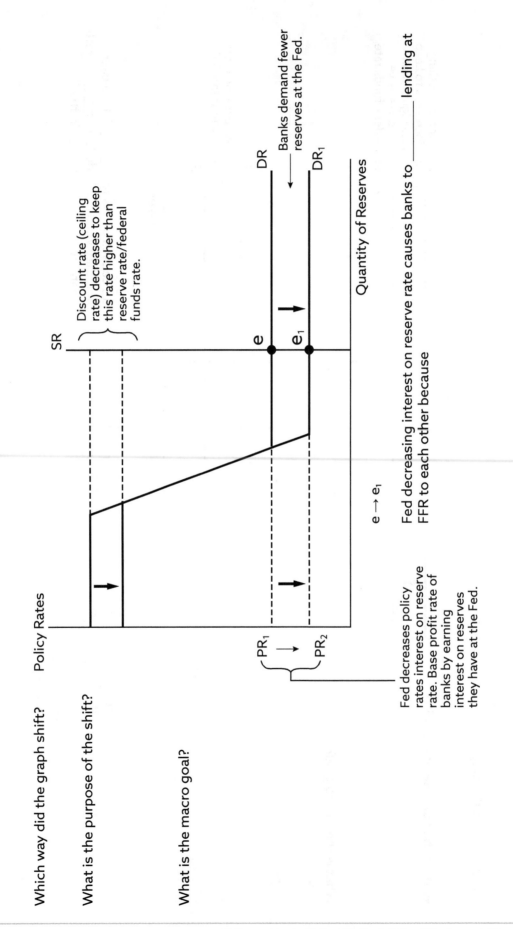

Which way did the graph shift?

What is the purpose of the shift?

What is the macro goal?

# Reviewing the Federal Reserve and Monetary Policy

## Part A

1.  How do the monetary powers of the Federal Reserve help it perform its functions of:

    (A)  The Nation's Central Bank

    (B)  The Bankers' Bank

2.  In a limited reserve system, why would Open Market Operations be the most frequently used monetary policy tool?

3.  In a limited reserve system (and prior to when banks were required to have required reserves), why would changing the required reserve rate be the least frequently used monetary policy tool?

4.  Due to the economic circumstances of the COVID 19 Pandemic and the existence of an ample reserve system, the Fed Board reduced reserve requirement ratios to zero percent effective March 26, 2020. What are the potential positives and negatives of removing required reserves from the banking system? Do you think it is more positive or more negative?

5.  Why would the discount rate be considered the ceiling rate of banks and the interest on reserve rate the floor rate for banks?

6.  How does the Federal Reserve have an indirect relationship with aggregate demand? Why doesn't it affect AD directly?

7.  Policy Analysis: How would you describe the difference between monetary and fiscal policy?

## Part B: Expansionary Response or Contractionary Response?

In the situations presented below, you must decide whether the appropriate policy response is Expansionary (E), Contractionary(C), or No Change (NC). Write E, C, or NC next to each of the following statements.

Once you have decided on the appropriate response, indicate what fiscal policy actions by Congress AND what Ample Reserve and Limited Reserve monetary policy actions taken by the Federal Reserve would be most appropriate.

____ 1. The economy is suffering from its worst slowdown in 30 years. Unemployment has reached 10%.

FISCAL RESPONSE _____

MONETARY RESPONSE _____

_____

____ 2. The annual inflation rate is 8.5% and rising.

FISCAL RESPONSE _____

MONETARY RESPONSE _____

_____

____ 3. Prices are dropping rapidly and inflation is at -4%. In other words, we are experiencing 4% deflation.

FISCAL RESPONSE _____

MONETARY RESPONSE _____

_____

____ 4. Inflation is at a steady 2% and unemployment is at 4%.

FISCAL RESPONSE _____

MONETARY RESPONSE _____

_____

____ 5. The annual rate of inflation is at 10% and rising and unemployment is also at 10% and rising.

FISCAL RESPONSE _____

MONETARY RESPONSE _____

_____

# UNIT 5
## LONG-RUN CONSEQUENCES OF STABILIZATION POLICIES

# UNIT 5 **MACROECONOMICS KEY IDEAS**

- In the short run, equilibrium levels of GDP can occur at less than, greater than, or equal to the full-employment level of GDP. The long-run equilibrium can occur only at full employment.

- Fiscal and monetary policy have short-run effects on macroeconomic outcomes.

- A Phillips curve illustrates the trade-off between inflation and unemployment. The trade-off differs in the short and long run, varies at different times, and is often different for increases and decreases in output. A Phillips curve is also used to illustrate how macroeconomic shocks affect inflation and unemployment.

- The short-run Phillips curve shows a trade-off between the inflation rate and the unemployment rate and is downward sloping. There is no trade-off between inflation and unemployment in the long run.

- The long-run Phillips curve is vertical. Long-run equilibrium corresponds to the intersection of the SRPC and the LRPC.

- Fiscal and monetary policy have long-run effects on macroeconomic outcomes. When the economy is at full employment, changes in the money supply have no effect on real output in the long run.

- Macroeconomic policy includes both fiscal and monetary policy. Both monetary and fiscal policies are primarily aggregate demand policies. Other economic policies are used to affect aggregate supply.

- Fiscal policy that changes taxes or government spending will affect the government's budget. When the government spends more than it taxes in a year, it creates a budget deficit. When the government taxes more than it spends in a year, it creates a budget surplus. The summation of the budget deficits and surpluses over time is the national debt. Deficits and debt have an effect on the macroeconomy.

- When a government is in a budget deficit, it will borrow to finance its spending. A loanable funds market model will show the effect of borrowing on the real interest rate and the crowding out of private investment.

- Crowding out is the effect on investment and consumption spending of an increase in interest rates caused by increased borrowing by the federal government. The higher interest rates crowd out business and consumer borrowing. Less economic growth is the result.

- Aggregate employment and aggregate output are directly related because firms need to employ more workers in order to produce more output, holding other factors constant. This is captured by the aggregate production function.

- Output per employed worker is a measure of average labor productivity. Productivity is determined by the level of technology and physical and human capital per worker.

- Supply-side fiscal policies affect aggregate demand, aggregate supply, and potential output in the short run and long run by influencing incentives that affect household and business economic behavior.

# UNIT 5 ACTIVITY 5-1.1

# Monetary and Fiscal Policy Interactions

In the figures accompanying each question, illustrate the short-run effects for each monetary and fiscal policy combination using the money market, the loanable funds market, and aggregate supply/aggregate demand (AS/AD) graph. Circle the up or down arrow (or ? for uncertain) and explain the effect of the policies on real gross domestic product (GDP), the price level, unemployment, interest rates, and investment.

1. The unemployment rate is 10 percent and the inflation rate is 2 percent. The federal government cuts personal income taxes and increases its spending. With "ample reserves," the Federal Reserve (the Fed) lowers the interest on reserve balance rate (IORB) it offers banks.

*Figure 5-1.1*
**EXPANSIONARY MONETARY AND FISCAL POLICY**

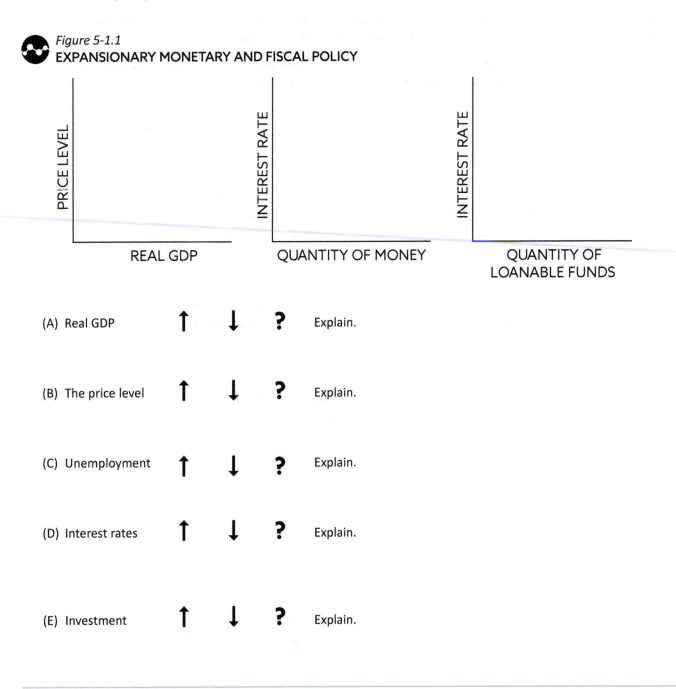

(A) Real GDP    ↑   ↓   ?    Explain.

(B) The price level    ↑   ↓   ?    Explain.

(C) Unemployment    ↑   ↓   ?    Explain.

(D) Interest rates    ↑   ↓   ?    Explain.

(E) Investment    ↑   ↓   ?    Explain.

   AP Macroeconomics Student Workbook © Council for Economic Education, New York, NY

2. The unemployment rate is 4 percent and the inflation rate is 9 percent. The federal government raises personal income taxes and cuts spending. With "ample reserves," the Fed raises the interest on reserve balance rate (IORB) it offers banks.

*Figure 5-1.2*
**CONTRACTIONARY MONETARY AND FISCAL POLICY**

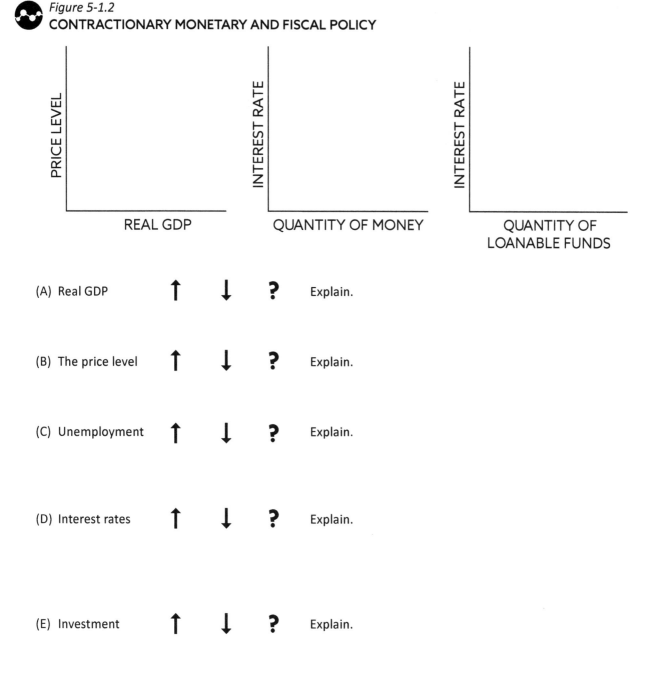

(A) Real GDP ↑ ↓ ? Explain.

(B) The price level ↑ ↓ ? Explain.

(C) Unemployment ↑ ↓ ? Explain.

(D) Interest rates ↑ ↓ ? Explain.

(E) Investment ↑ ↓ ? Explain.

3.  The unemployment rate is 7 percent and the inflation rate is 7 percent. The federal government cuts personal income taxes and maintains current spending. With "ample reserves," the Fed raises the interest on reserve balance rate (IORB) it offers banks.

*Figure 5-1.3*
**CONTRACTIONARY MONETARY POLICY AND EXPANSIONARY FISCAL POLICY**

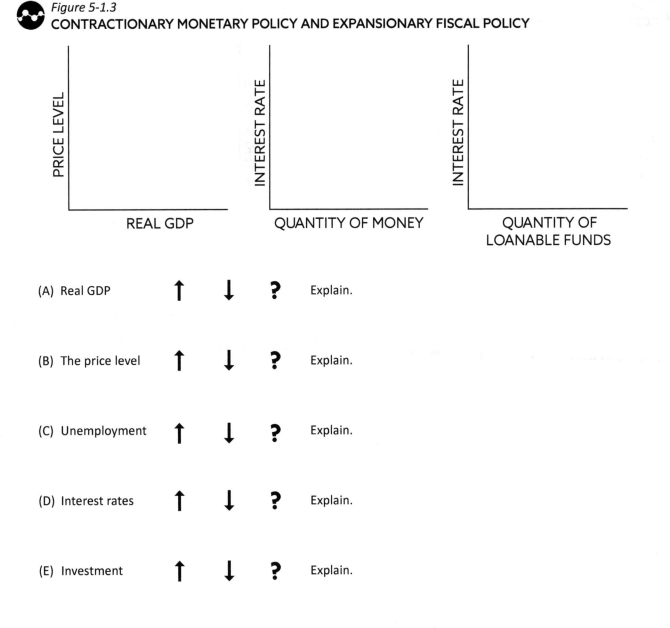

(A)  Real GDP        ↑   ↓   **?**    Explain.

(B)  The price level  ↑   ↓   **?**    Explain.

(C)  Unemployment   ↑   ↓   **?**    Explain.

(D)  Interest rates   ↑   ↓   **?**    Explain.

(E)  Investment      ↑   ↓   **?**    Explain.

# Money Growth and Inflation

The relationship among money, price, and real output can be represented by the equation of exchange, which typically takes the following form:

$$MV = PQ$$

where

> **M = the money supply**
> **V = the velocity of money (the number of times an average dollar bill is spent)**
> **P = the average price level**
> **Q = real value of all final goods and services (real gross domestic product [GDP])**

This equation shows the balance between "money," represented on the left side of the equation, and goods and services, represented on the right side of the equation. The equation shows that, for a given level of V, if M increases more than Q there must be an increase in P (inflation) to keep the two sides of the equation equal. This means that an increase in the money supply not offset by an increase in real output will lead to inflation. Classical economists assumed that the velocity of money was stable (constant) over time because institutional factors – such as how frequently people are paid – largely determine velocity. Therefore, changes in the money supply will lead to inflation if the economy is at full employment.

1. Define (in your own words and in one or two sentences each) the four variables in the equation of exchange.

2. The product of V and M equals PQ. What is PQ?

3.  Suppose velocity remains constant, while the money supply increases. Explain how this would affect nominal GDP if the economy were at full employment. Show this explanation on the graph in Figure 5-2.1. Label full employment equilibrium as Point A, the new equilibrium as Point B, and show/label the inflationary gap.

*Figure 5-2.1*
**INFLATIONARY GAP**

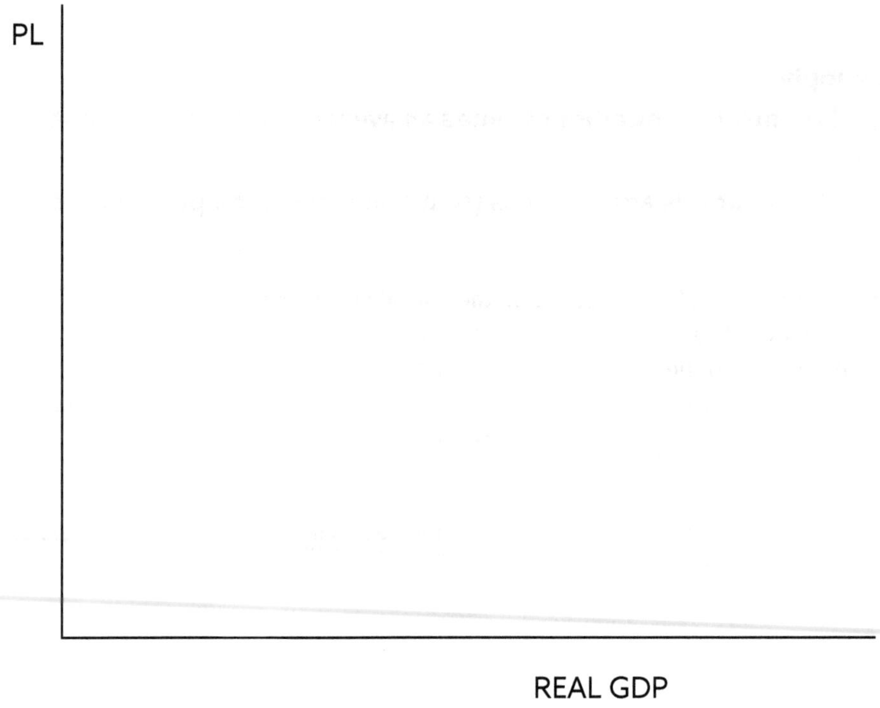

PL

REAL GDP

4.  Changes in technology have led to increases in electronic transactions. Explain how these changes affect velocity.

# Government Deficits and the National Debt

The two primary tools of discretionary fiscal policy are government spending (G) and taxes (T). When the government conducts expansionary fiscal policy to counteract recession, G increases and/or T decreases. When G increases and/or T decreases, the government budget moves toward a larger deficit or a smaller surplus.

The effect of government borrowing can be modeled using the loanable funds market. A government budget deficit results in an increase in the demand (D) for loanable funds. A budget surplus reduces the demand for loanable funds. It results in an increase in the supply (S) of loanable funds if the government pays off the debt.

1.  Complete Table 5-3.1. In each column, place an up arrow for increase, a down arrow for decrease, or NC for no change.

*Table 5-3.1*
**BUDGET EFFECTS OF FISCAL POLICY**

| Fiscal policy | Tools of fiscal policy | Effect on government's budget | Effect on debt | Effect on real interest rate |
|---|---|---|---|---|
| Expansionary | G __ T __ | Deficit __ OR Surplus __ | | |
| Contractionary | G __ T __ | Deficit __ OR Surplus __ | | |

2. The central bank of a country with limited reserves can counteract the effect of budget deficits on the real interest rate by conducting an open market purchase of government securities. When the central bank purchases the securities directly from the government, this is referred to as monetizing the debt and is seen as highly inflationary. The effect of an open-market purchase of government securities can be modeled using the money market.

   Draw a graph of the money market showing how an open-market purchase of government securities affects the nominal interest rate.

INTEREST RATE

QUANTITY OF MONEY

3. How would the change in the nominal interest rate affect the real interest rate? Explain.

4. Why is monetizing the debt inflationary?

# Crowding Out

Expansionary fiscal policy increases aggregate demand and moves the budget toward deficit. If deficit spending is financed through borrowing, the government will demand loanable funds. The government's demand for loanable funds ($D_{lf}$) added to the demand for loanable funds by private borrowers. Thus, expansionary fiscal policy increases $D_{lf}$ and may cause interest rates to rise. Because the government is borrowing money to finance its expansionary fiscal policy, consumers and businesses will be "crowded out" of financial markets. If consumers and businesses are not able to borrow to finance spending, it will lead to a decrease in aggregate demand (AD).

*Figure 5-4.1*
**CROWDING OUT**

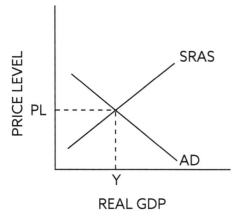
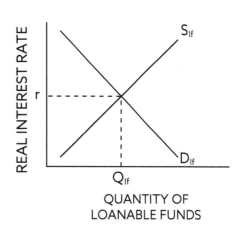

1. Assume fiscal policy is expansionary and the government funds the resulting deficit through borrowing. In Figure 5-4.1, shift one curve in each graph to illustrate the effect of the fiscal policy, and label the new equilibrium values.

2. How will the change in the equilibrium interest rate in the loanable funds market affect the short run aggregate supply (SRAS) curve in the long run? Show on the AS/AD graph above, and explain.

# Short-Run Phillips Curve

Student Alert: Pay close attention to the axes when you graph Phillips curves!

1.  Assume the economy begins at long-run equilibrium as shown in Figure 5-5.1 below. Graph the effect on the equilibrium price level (PL) and real GDP (Y) if there is a decrease in aggregate demand (AD). Label the equilibrium price level and real GDP after the decrease in aggregate demand as $PL_2$ and $Y_2$.

*Figure 5-5.1*
**AGGREGATE DEMAND DECREASE**

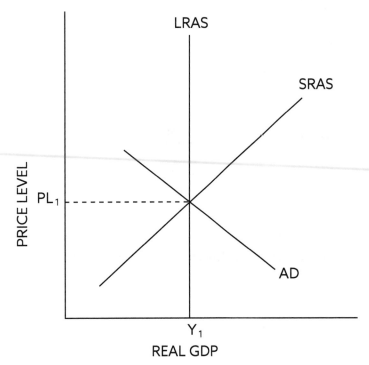

2.  What happens to each of the following in the short run?

    Real GDP _____ The unemployment rate _____

    The price level _____ Real wages _____

3.  Draw a graph of a short-run Phillips curve below. Make sure you label your axes correctly. You will plot $P_1$ and $P_2$ along with their corresponding unemployment rates. There are no numbers for $P_1$ and $P_2$, just plot $P_1$ at some level and then plot $P_2$ either above or below it, as shown in the graph above. Then select some unemployment rate ($U_1$) to go with $P_1$ and then plot $U_2$ either above or below $U_1$ as shown on the graph above. Since the short-run Phillips curve shows the relationship between the inflation rate and the unemployment rate and the aggregate demand/aggregate supply (AD/AS) graph shows the relationship between the price level and real GDP, you need to determine how the change in aggregate demand affects the unemployment rate when the output level changes. Remember that when the economy is in long-run equilibrium, it is at full employment (the unemployment rate is low), and as real GDP falls, the decrease in production causes employment to decrease the unemployment rate to increase.

INFLATION RATE

UNEMPLOYMENT RATE

When the economy of the 1970s experienced high inflation and high unemployment at the same time (i.e., stagflation) the Phillips curve relationship no longer appeared to be true. Eventually, additional data showed that the negative relationship between the inflation rate and the unemployment rate still held, but that the short-run Phillips curve had shifted to the right, as shown in Figure 5-5.2 below.

The rightward shift of the short-run Phillips curve was due to a negative supply shock – a decrease in aggregate supply caused by an increase in the price of oil. A positive supply shock (e.g., an advance in technology) will shift the short-run Phillips curve to the left. A negative (positive) supply shock means that for every given unemployment rate, the corresponding inflation rate is higher (lower).

*Figure 5-5.2*
**SHORT-RUN PHILLIPS CURVES**

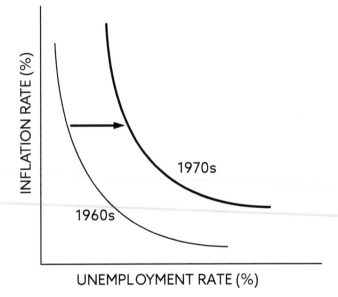

4.  Assume the economy begins at long-run equilibrium as shown in Figure 5-5.3 below. Draw a new SRAS curve illustrating the effect of an increase in oil prices. Label the new curve SRAS2, the new equilibrium price level $PL_2$, and the new level of real GDP $Y_2$.

*Figure 5-5.3*
**EFFECT OF AN INCREASE IN OIL PRICES**

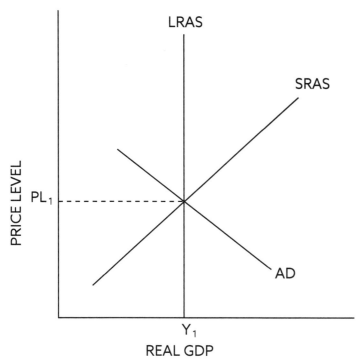

5.  Based on your graph, what happens to each of the following in the short run?

    Real GDP _____ The unemployment rate _____

    The price level _____ Real wages _____

    Supply shocks are not the only thing that will shift the short-run Phillips curve. The expected rate of inflation will also cause the short-run Phillips curve to shift. When workers expect inflation they bargain for higher wage rates, and employers are more willing to grant higher wage rates when they expect to sell their product for higher prices in the future.

    When the expected rate of inflation is higher, the short-run Phillips curve shifts to the right, and the actual rate of inflation increases. If the expected rate of inflation decreases, the short-run Phillips curve will shift to the left and the actual inflation rate will decrease. Expectations for inflation lead to a change in actual inflation – like a self-fulfilling prophecy.

# The Long-Run Phillips Curve and the Role of Expectations

## Part A: Expectation and the Short-Run Phillips Curve

The short-run Phillips curve (SRPC) is drawn for a given expected rate of inflation and a specific natural rate of unemployment. Changes in inflationary expectations will shift the SRPC. People base their inflationary expectations on information and personal experience, which can result in gaps between the expected rate of inflation and the actual rate of inflation.

1.  Suppose the economy is experiencing 2 percent inflation. News of rising energy costs increases people's expectations of inflation. Graph the change in the SRPC.

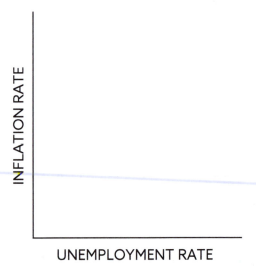

2.  If the government increases spending, how does it affect inflationary expectations? Explain.

3.  If people are confident that a new Federal Reserve policy will achieve and maintain price stability, how does it affect inflationary expectations? Explain.

4.  What will happen to the actual rate of inflation if people expect a higher inflation rate in the future? What will happen to the actual rate of inflation if people expect a lower inflation rate in the future? Explain.

## Part B: The Long-Run Phillips Curve

The long-run Phillips curve (LRPC) represents the relationship between unemployment and inflation after the economy has adjusted to inflationary expectations. The LRPC corresponds to the long-run aggregate supply (LRAS) and occurs at the non-accelerating inflation rate of unemployment (NAIRU). The NAIRU corresponds to the full employment level of output and the natural rate of unemployment. Trying to keep the unemployment rate below the NAIRU leads to accelerating inflation rates and cannot be maintained in the long run. Unemployment rates above NAIRU will lead to accelerating deflation that cannot be maintained.

The LRPC is vertical because any unemployment rate above or below the NAIRU cannot be maintained. This means that there is no long-run trade-off between inflation and unemployment – that is, no policy can maintain unemployment rates below the NAIRU in the long run.

5. Draw a graph of the LRPC. Be sure to correctly label the axes and label the point at which the LRPC intersects the horizontal axis.

6. What does the slope of the LRPC indicate about the trade-off between the inflation rate and the unemployment rate?

7. Use the graph in problem 1 to show the effect on the LRPC if the natural rate of unemployment decreases. Label the new curve LRPC$_1$. What happens to the LRAS when the natural rate of unemployment decreases?

*Figure 5-5.4*
**LONG-RUN ADJUSTMENT**

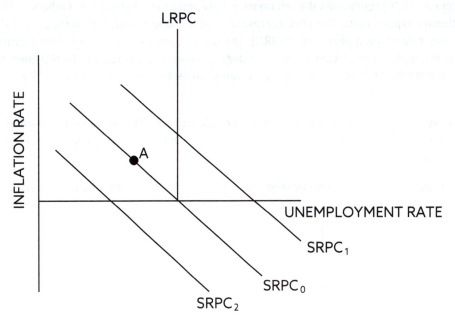

8.  What change in inflationary expectations is shown by the shift in the short-run Phillips curve (SRPC) from $SRPC_0$ to $SRPC_1$ in Figure 5-5.4?

9.  The LRPC is vertical at the unemployment rate that corresponds to an inflation rate equal to zero. What is the name for this rate of unemployment?

10. At point A on the graph in Figure 5-5.4, the actual rate of inflation is (greater than/less than) the expected rate of inflation, which will cause the SRPC to shift to the (right/left).

11. Label point B on the graph where the economy will be in long-run equilibrium after the change in inflationary expectations noted in Q #8.

12. Label point C on the graph where the economy will be if policy makers attempt to keep the unemployment rate where it was at point A after the change in inflationary expectations.

# Economic Growth

## Long-Run Aggregate Supply and the Production Possibilities Curve

The long-run aggregate supply (LRAS) curve is vertical at the full-employment level of output. This means that LRAS doesn't change as the price level changes. The location of the LRAS depends on the productive capacity of the economy. Developing more/better resources or improving technology will shift the LRAS curve outward.

The LRAS curve represents a point on an economy's production possibilities curve (PPC). Remember that the PPC represents the maximum output that can be produced given scarce resources. The economy grows if the PPC shifts outward because of more/better resources or technological advances. For the same reason, the LRAS curve shifts outward with more/better resources or if there are technological advances.

Aggregate output in the economy can actually be greater than LRAS in the short run. This means that resources are being used more intensively. For example, workers can work double hours in the short run. However, they can't continue to work that number of hours in the long run. Eventually, the equilibrium level of output will always return to the full-employment level. Aggregate output can only increase in the long run if the LRAS has increased.

> Student Alert: Make sure you don't confuse real gross domestic product (GDP) changes in the short run due to business cycles with long-run economic growth!

# UNIT 5 **ACTIVITY 5-6.1** (continued)

Use the graphs in Figure 5-6.1 to answer the questions that follow.

*Figure 5-6.1*
## AGGREGATE SUPPLY AND PRODUCTION POSSIBILITIES CURVES

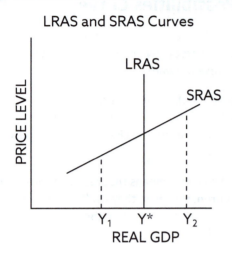

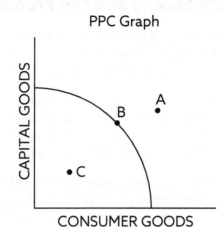

1.  What does a PPC show? What are the assumptions about resources and technology in the PPC model?

2.  List two things that could happen to allow the economy to produce at Point A.

3.  In Figure 5-6.1, $Y^*$, $Y_1$, and $Y_2$ on the aggregate supply graph correspond to which points on the PPC graph? Explain.

    $Y^* \rightarrow$ Point ____

    $Y1 \rightarrow$ Point ____

    $Y2 \rightarrow$ Point ____

4.  List two things that could happen to allow the economy to produce $Y_2$ output.

5.  How can the economy produce at $Y_2$ in the short run? If it is produced at $Y_2$ in the short run, what will happen in the long run? Explain.

# Measuring Economic Growth in Hamilton County and Jefferson County

1. Use Table 5-6.1 to fill out Tables 5-6.2, 5-6.3, and 5-6.4. Recall that a percentage change is equal to the change divided by the starting value.

 *Table 5-6.1*

| Year | Hamilton real GDP | Hamilton population | Jefferson real GDP | Jefferson population |
|---|---|---|---|---|
| 1 | $2.1 billion | 70,000 | $500,000 | 15 |
| 2 | $2.5 billion | 80,000 | $525,000 | 16 |
| 3 | $2.8 billion | 90,000 | $600,000 | 17 |
| 4 | $2.7 billion | 86,000 | $650,000 | 18 |

 *Table 5-6.2*

| Time period | Hamilton % change in real GDP | Jefferson % change in real GDP |
|---|---|---|
| From Year 1 to Year 2 | 19.0% | 5.0% |
| From Year 2 to Year 3 | | |
| From Year 3 to Year 4 | | |

 *Table 5-6.3*

| Year | Hamilton per capita real GDP | Jefferson per capita real GDP |
|---|---|---|
| 1 | $30,000.00 | $33,333.33 |
| 2 | | |
| 3 | | |
| 4 | | |

 *Table 5-6.4*

| Time period | Hamilton % change in per capita real GDP | Jefferson % change in per capita real GDP |
|---|---|---|
| From Year 1 to Year 2 | 4.17% | –1.56% |
| From Year 2 to Year 3 | | |
| From Year 3 to Year 4 | | |

2. When did Hamilton County experience the largest growth in real GDP?

   (A) When did Hamilton County experience the largest growth in per capita real GDP?

   (B) Why are these growth rates different?

3. When did Jefferson County experience the largest growth in real GDP?

   (A) When did Jefferson County experience the largest growth in per capita real GDP?

   (B) Why are these growth rates different?

4. Which county do you believe is better off? Explain.

## Analyzing Economic Growth

5. Economic growth can be illustrated using both the LRAS curve and the PPC. Illustrate that economic growth on the following graphs.

PRICE LEVEL

REAL GDP

CAPITAL GOODS

CONSUMPTION GOODS

# Public Policy and Economic Growth

## Part A

A country experiences economic growth if it has increased its long-run ability to produce goods and services, no matter the current short-run phase of the nation's business cycle. Recall that short-run fluctuations in the business cycle are caused by changes in either aggregate demand or short-run aggregate supply. These short-run changes lead to increases, or decreases, in real gross domestic product (GDP). However, these changes are movements around the long-run stability of full-employment GDP. So, another way to think about economic growth is to consider the level of real GDP when the nation is at full employment. If this level of full-employment output, as seen by the location of the long-run aggregate supply curve in Figure 5-7.1, is increasing, the nation is experiencing real growth.

Using the production possibilities model, economic growth is shown as an outward movement of the production possibilities curve, as shown in Figure 5-7.1. This allows a nation to produce combinations of goods and services that were previously unattainable, given the nation's stock of resources and technology.

*Figure 5-7.1*
**LONG-RUN ECONOMIC GROWTH**

Does each of the following policies lead to economic growth? State yes or no and explain.

1. The government provides subsidies and tax incentives for firms to research new, more efficient, technology in production.

2.  With renewed emphasis on education, the nation's high school graduation rate increases from 70 percent to 85 percent, and the literacy rate rises from 98 percent to 99.5 percent.

3.  The central bank expands the money supply in an attempt to boost spending and recover from a recession.

4.  Because the nation is experiencing unusually low rates of spending and high unemployment, the government lowers household income tax rates and increases military spending.

## Government Policies to Promote Long-Run Economic Growth

The key to economic growth is the productivity of the nation where productivity is commonly measured as the quantity of goods and services produced from each unit of labor. The following factors contribute to a nation's productivity, and thus its economic growth.

5.  How will each of the following policies affect economic growth and why?

    (A)  The government raises taxes on businesses.

    (B)  The government invests in improvements to the national highway system.

    (C)  Research and development leads to improvements in technology.

    (D)  Labor productivity increases as a result of a new education initiative.

    (E)  Expansionary economic policy leads to lower interest rates.

    (F)  A country's government is unable to enforce property rights and the country is on the verge of a civil war.

    (G)  Government agencies establish regulations to maintain natural resources at sustainable levels.

6.  Draw an aggregate demand and aggregate supply (AS/AD) graph to show the U.S. economy in long-run equilibrium.

    (A)  Suppose the U.S. economy experiences increased productivity. Show the short-run impact on your graph.

PRICE

REAL GDP

    (B)  Now suppose that these increased productivity gains last into the long run and create real economic growth in the United States. Show the long-run impact of this growth on real GDP and the price level in the graph.

PRICE

REAL GDP

## Part B

7.  Underline the actions that would be considered supply-side policies. (There might be more than one answer.)

    (A) Removing markets from competition

    (B) Increasing interest rates

    (C) Reducing regulations relating to increasing employment

    (D) Reducing income taxes to increase aggregate demand

    (E) Imposing credit controls to limit borrowing

    ---
    Student Alert: It is important to understand that monetary policies are not targeted to aggregate supply.

    ---

8.  What supply-side policy might be used by the government to lower unemployment?

    (A) Decrease government spending

    (B) Increase interest rates

    (C) Buy bonds

    (D) Increase taxes

    (E) Decrease taxes

9.  The SRAS slopes (upward/downward). In the (short run/long run), businesses respond to price increases by supplying more, but in the (short run/long run) these businesses may not respond to an increase in prices. In the short run, changes like a tax increase will shift the SRAS curve to the (left/right), where a reduction in employment costs and wages would shift the SRAS curve to the (left/right).

# UNIT 6
## AN OPEN ECONOMY: INTERNATIONAL TRADE AND FINANCE

# UNIT 6 **MACROECONOMICS KEY IDEAS**

- A country's balance of payments accounts are a summary of all of the country's transactions with other countries.

- There are two important accounts within the balance of payments: the *current account* and the *capital* and *financial account* (formerly known as the *capital account*). The current account records a country's exports and imports of goods and services, net investment income, and net transfers. The financial account records the difference between a country's sale of assets to foreigners and its purchase of assets from foreigners.

- The current account includes the country's trade balance (net exports).

- The capital and financial account (CFA) measures capital inflows in the form of foreign savings that finance domestic investment and government borrowing.

- The current account and the financial account must sum to zero.

- Capital flows between countries occur when the loanable funds markets in the two countries establish different equilibrium real interest rates. Financial capital will flow into the country where the real interest rate is higher.

- Trade barriers such as tariffs and quotas limit the gains from trade. These barriers generally protect domestic sellers at the expense of domestic buyers.

- To trade, nations must exchange currencies.

- An exchange rate is the price of one currency in terms of another. Foreign exchange markets use supply and demand to set exchange rates.

- Appreciation is an increase in the value of a nation's currency in foreign exchange markets. Appreciation of a nation's currency decreases exports and increases imports.

- Depreciation is a decrease in the value of a nation's currency in foreign exchange markets. Depreciation of a nation's currency increases exports and decreases imports.

- Monetary and fiscal policies can affect exchange rates, the international balance of trade, and the balance of payments.

- Domestic economic policies affect international trade, and international trade affects the domestic economy. The international sector influences unemployment, inflation, and economic growth.

- Factors that shift the demand for a currency (such as the demand for that country's goods, services, or assets) and the supply of a currency (such as tariffs or quotas on the other country's goods and services) change the equilibrium exchange rate.

- Fiscal policy can influence aggregate demand, real output, the price level, and exchange rates.

- The demand for a currency in a foreign exchange market arises from the demand for the country's goods, services, and financial assets and shows the inverse relationship between the exchange rate and the quantity demanded of a currency.

- The supply of a currency in a foreign exchange market arises from making payments in other currencies and shows the positive relationship between the exchange rate and the quantity supplied of a currency.

- Monetary policy can influence aggregate demand, real output, the price level, and interest rates, and thereby affect exchange rates.

- In an open economy, differences in real interest rates across countries change the relative values of domestic and foreign assets. Financial capital will flow toward the country with the relatively higher interest rate.

- Central banks can influence the domestic interest rate in the short run, which in turn will affect net capital inflows.

---

# Barriers to Trade

1.  Graph the "Total Supply with Tariff" curve and indicate the amount of the tariff on the graph. Label the new equilibrium price and quantity after the tariff as $P_T$ and $Q_T$ on the graph.

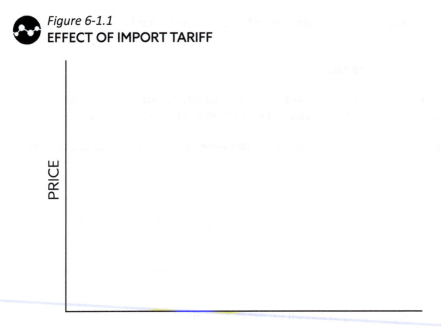

*Figure 6-1.1*
**EFFECT OF IMPORT TARIFF**

PRICE

QUANTITY

2.  What is the effect of the tariff on the equilibrium price and quantity for domestic consumers and domestic producers compared with the free trade levels?

*Figure 6-1.2*
**EFFECT OF IMPORT QUOTA**

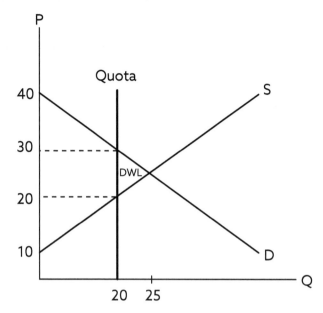

3.  Use Figure 6-1.2 to determine the effect of a quota. What is the effect of the quota on the equilibrium price and quantity for domestic consumers and domestic producers? Why is the line vertical? What is the significance of the Deadweight Loss?

4.  Identify the arguments frequently used to impose some type of trade barrier. Discuss the pros and cons of three arguments.

# Balance of Payments Accounts

Evaluate each of the transactions on the U.S. balance of payments and complete Table 6-2.1. Check either debit or credit, and current account or financial account.

*Table 6-2.1*
**TRANSACTIONS ON THE US BALANCE OF PAYMENTS**

| | Credit + | Debit − | Current account | Capital and financial account |
|---|---|---|---|---|
| 1. Harley-Davidson USA purchases $25 million in production machinery from a Japanese company. | | | | |
| 2. André Prenoor, U.S. entrepreneur, invests $50 million to develop a theme park in Malaysia. | | | | |
| 3. A Chinese company sells $1 million worth of berets to the U.S. Army. | | | | |
| 4. BMW pays $1 million to a U.S. shipper for transporting cars from Germany to the United States. | | | | |
| 5. Each month, Ima Grent, who recently arrived in the United States, sends half her paycheck to her sister in Poland. | | | | |
| 6. Bank of America pays $5 million in interest to French depositors. | | | | |
| 7. Senor Ramos from Spain buys a shopping center in Florida. | | | | |
| 8. A Brazilian investor buys five $10,000 U.S. Treasury bonds. | | | | |
| 9. German tourists spend $3 million in the United States; U.S. tourists spend $5 million in Germany. | | | | |
| 10. Sam Boney, U.S. ice-rink magnate, buys stock in a Chilean ice-rink chain. | | | | |

# Calculating the Balance of Payments

1. Year-End Balance of Payments, Z-Land

   **Current Account**

   | | | |
   |---|---|---|
   | Z-Land exports of goods | $ +300 | |
   | Z-Land imports of goods | -400 | |
   | Z-Land exports of services | +150 | |
   | Z-Land imports of services | -120 | |
   | Balance of trade | _____ | |
   | Net investment income | +10 | |
   | Net transfers | -14 | |
   | Balance on current account | | _____ |

   **Capital and Financial Account**

   | | | |
   |---|---|---|
   | Z-Land capital going abroad | -110 | |
   | Foreign capital coming into Z-Land | +160 | |

   **Official Reserves Account**

   | | | |
   |---|---|---|
   | Official reserves transactions balance | _____ | |
   | Balance on capital and financial account | | _____ |
   | **Total** | | $ _____ |

2. Does Z-Land have a current account deficit or surplus? How do you know?

# Graphing Loanable Funds and the Current Account

It is important to understand that the *current account balance* and the *capital* and *financial account balance must sum to zero*. Consider the example of a country that imports more than it exports and runs a current account deficit. A surplus in the capital and financial account must offset the current account deficit because the net imports must either be paid for or purchased on credit. That is, the foreign currency used to buy the net imports had to come from somewhere. A capital and financial account surplus must exist to supply the needed foreign currency if there is a current account deficit. In other words, a *current account deficit* must come from a capital and financial account surplus and vice versa.

> Student Alert: Changes in the capital and financial account impact the market for loanable funds, not the money market.
>
>

Assume there are only two countries, country A and country B.

1. If Country A is running a current account surplus, what must be true of Country A's capital and financial account? Explain.

2. Draw a graph of the loanable funds market in Country B and show how an increase in Country A's current account surplus affects the supply of loanable funds and the equilibrium interest rate. Make sure you label all axes and curves.

# Exchange Rates

Use the data in Table 6-3.1 to calculate the cost of the following products in U.S. dollars. To solve, divide the cost of the product in the foreign currency by the cost of the U.S. dollar in the foreign currency.

Indicate whether the dollar has appreciated or depreciated between May and August.

> Student Alert: Remember that to solve, divide the cost of the product in the foreign currency by the cost of the U.S. dollar in the foreign currency.

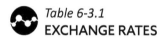

Table 6-3.1
**EXCHANGE RATES**

|  | Cost of foreign currency in U.S. dollars (U.S. dollars/foreign currency) | | Cost of U.S. dollar in foreign currency (foreign currency/U.S. dollars) | |
|---|---|---|---|---|
|  | May | August | May | August |
| British pound | 1.4 | 1.8 | 0.71 | 0.56 |
| Canadian dollar | 0.64 | 0.63 | 1.5625 | 1.5873 |
| European euro | 0.87 | 0.91 | 1.149 | 1.099 |
| Brazilian real | 0.205 | 0.199 | 4.87 | 5.02 |
| Japanese yen | 0.0083 | 0.0090 | 120.482 | 111.111 |
| Mexican peso | 0.1101 | 0.1502 | 9.083 | 6.6558 |

Table 6-3.2
**PRODUCTS TO CALCULATE EXCHANGE RATES**

|  | May | August | Appreciated or Depreciated? |
|---|---|---|---|
| 1. A dinner for two that costs 500 Mexican pesos |  |  |  |
| 2. A hotel room that costs 30,000 Japanese yen |  |  |  |
| 3. A BMW that costs 85,000 euros in Germany |  |  |  |
| 4. A pound of Brazilian coffee beans that costs 130 real |  |  |  |
| 5. A pair of pants that costs 72 pounds in London |  |  |  |
| 6. A leather jacket that costs 360 Canadian dollars |  |  |  |

7.  Imagine you're planning a dream trip abroad and suddenly the exchange rate for your currency takes a wild swing and depreciates a great deal. How would this roller-coaster of exchange rates impact your travel plans and spending choices? Explain and give examples. Would you rather the dollar be appreciating or depreciating? Explain why.

# Graphing the Foreign Exchange Market

Consider the following situations. In each case, an underlying event causes a change in foreign exchange markets. Graph the effect on the equilibrium exchange rate and currency exchanged in the foreign exchange markets.

> Student Alert: Pay close attention to correct labeling on foreign exchange market graphs!

## French tourists flock to Mexico's beaches.

*Figure 6-4.3*
FRENCH TOURISTS VISIT MEXICO

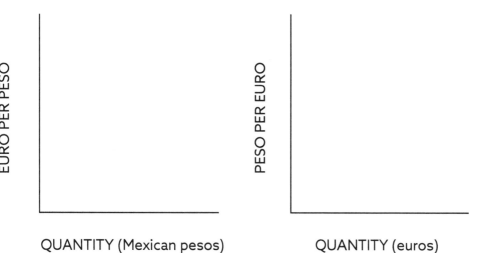

QUANTITY (Mexican pesos)          QUANTITY (euros)

1. Why did the curves shift? Which currency is appreciating and which currency is depreciating?

---

**Japanese video games have become popular with U.S. children.**

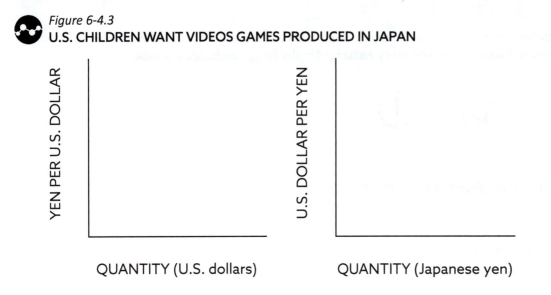

*Figure 6-4.3*
U.S. CHILDREN WANT VIDEOS GAMES PRODUCED IN JAPAN

2. Why did the curves shift? Which currency is appreciating and which currency is depreciating?

**Real interest rates in the United States rise faster than real interest rates in Canada.**

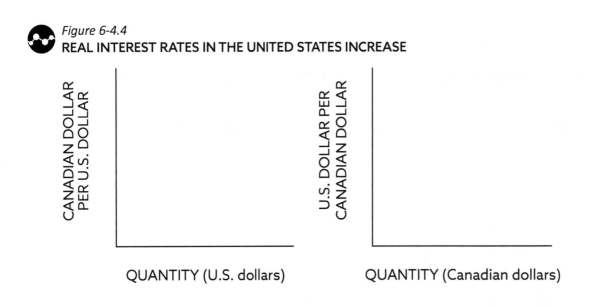

*Figure 6-4.4*
REAL INTEREST RATES IN THE UNITED STATES INCREASE

3. Why did the curves shift? Which currency is appreciating and which currency is depreciating?

# Policies and Economic Conditions Affect Exchange Rates

Changes in a nation's monetary and fiscal policies affect its exchange rates and its balance of trade through the real interest rate, income, and the price level. Changes in the value of a country's currency affect the balance of trade, which affects aggregate demand. Changes in aggregate demand affect real output and the price level. In other words, domestic policies influence currency values, and currency values influence domestic policies. Policy makers cannot ignore the international effects of changes in monetary and fiscal policies.

For each scenario, show the effect on equilibrium exchange rate and quantity of currency in the foreign exchange market graphs in Figures 6-5.1 through 6-5.5. Use the graphs to show the starting equilibrium exchange rate and equilibrium quantity of currency, the shift that occurs, and the new equilibrium exchange rate and quantity. Following each set of graphs, indicate the short-run effect of the change in the foreign exchange market on net exports, aggregate demand, and the price level in the United States. (Ignore the effects on the financial account, that comes next.)

*Figure 6-5.1*
**JAPAN'S REAL GDP INCREASES**

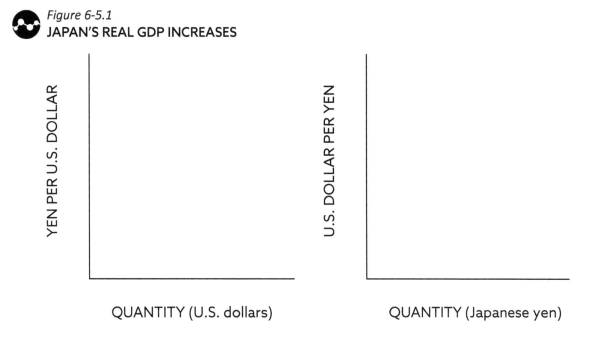

1. Effect if Japan's real gross domestic product (GDP) increases:

   Rationale:

   (A) U.S. imports (increase/decrease). Explain.

(B) U.S. exports (increase/decrease). Explain.

(C) U.S. aggregate demand (increases/decreases). Explain.

(D) The price level in the United States (increases/decreases). Explain.

*Figure 6-5.2*
**REAL INTEREST RATES IN THE UNITED STATES INCREASE RELATIVE TO GREAT BRITAIN**

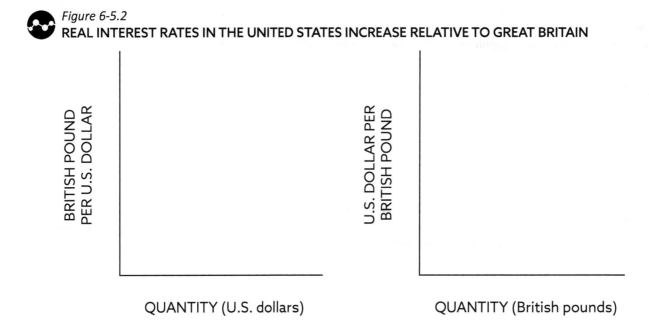

2. Effect if real interest rates in the United States increase relative to Great Britain:

   Rationale:

   (A) U.S. imports (increase/decrease). Explain.

   (B) U.S. exports (increase/decrease). Explain.

   (C) U.S. aggregate demand (increases/decreases). Explain.

   (D) The price level in the United States (increases/decreases). Explain.

*Figure 6-5.3*
**EUROPE EXPERIENCES A RECESSION**

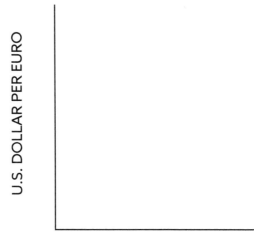

EURO PER U.S. DOLLAR

QUANTITY (U.S. dollars)

U.S. DOLLAR PER EURO

QUANTITY (euros)

3. Effect if Europe experiences a recession:

Rationale:

(A) U.S. imports (increase/decrease). Explain.

(B) U.S. exports (increase/decrease). Explain.

(C) U.S. aggregate demand (increases/decreases). Explain.

(D) The price level in the United States (increases/decreases). Explain.

*Figure 6-5.4*
**THE PRICE LEVEL IN CANADA INCREASES RELATIVE TO THE UNITED STATES**

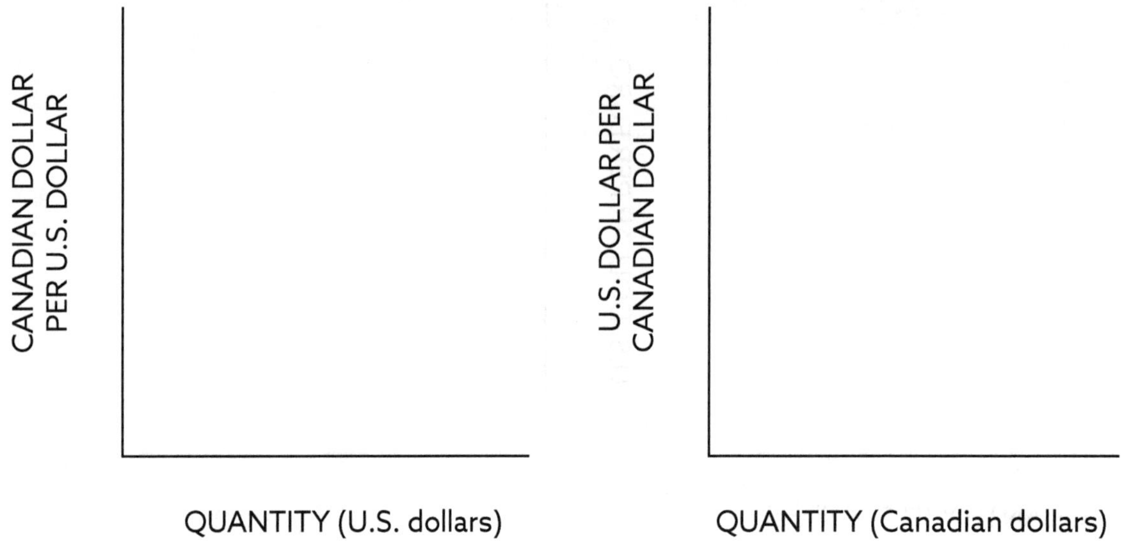
CANADIAN DOLLAR PER U.S. DOLLAR
QUANTITY (U.S. dollars)
U.S. DOLLAR PER CANADIAN DOLLAR
QUANTITY (Canadian dollars)

4. Effect if the price level in Canada increases relative to the United States:

   Rationale:

   (A) U.S. imports (increase/decrease). Explain.

   (B) U.S. exports (increase/decrease). Explain.

   (C) U.S. aggregate demand (increases/decreases). Explain.

   (D) The price level in the United States (increases/decreases). Explain.

*Figure 6-5.5*
**EFFECT ON TAIWAN IF U.S. GOVERNMENT DECREASES TAXES**

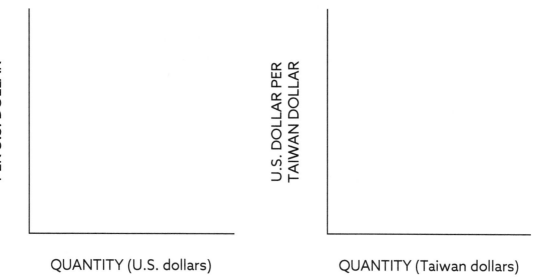

5.  Effect on Taiwan if U.S. government decreases taxes:
    Rationale:

    (A)  U.S. imports (increase/decrease). Explain.

    (B)  U.S. exports (increase/decrease). Explain.

    (C)  U.S. aggregate demand (increases/decreases). Explain.

    (D)  The price level in the United States (increases/decreases). Explain.

# UNIT 6 **ACTIVITY 6-6.1**

# Changes on the Foreign Exchange Market and Net Exports

The term capital flow refers to the movement of financial capital (money) between economies. Capital inflows consist of foreign funds moving into an economy from another country; capital outflows, or capital flight is the opposite – domestic funds moving out of an economy to another country. For example, from the perspective of the U.S. economy, the construction of a new plant by a Japanese automobile manufacturer within the United States is an example of capital inflow. Likewise, when an American manufacturer finances the construction of a plant outside of the United States, it is an example of capital outflow.

## Capital Flows Resulting from a Change in Net Exports

1.  Japanese firms have recently increased their imports of American made semiconductors. As a result, the U.S. current account moves toward (surplus/deficit) and U.S. net exports will (increase/decrease).

2.  Illustrate on the graphs provided how the relative exchange rates of the U.S. dollar and Japanese yen will change as a result of the increase in Japanese purchases of U.S. semiconductors. Be sure to label your graphs correctly (e.g., the price of dollars should be stated in terms of yen per dollar, and vice versa).

**RELATIVE EXCHANGE RATES OF THE US DOLLAR AND JAPANESE YEN**

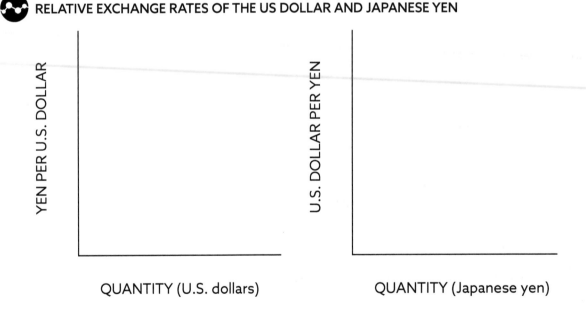

QUANTITY (U.S. dollars)          QUANTITY (Japanese yen)

 AP Macroeconomics Student Workbook © Council for Economic Education, New York, NY

3.  Great Britain was a leading investor in American firms at this time. Use correctly labeled graphs of the markets for dollars and pounds to illustrate the relative change in value of these two currencies on the foreign exchange market as a result of British investment in American companies. Be sure to label your graphs correctly (e.g., the price of dollars should be stated in terms of pounds per dollar, and vice versa).

*Figure 6-6.2*
**FOREIGN EXCHANGE MARKET AS A RESULT OF BRITISH INVESTMENT IN AMERICAN COMPANIES**

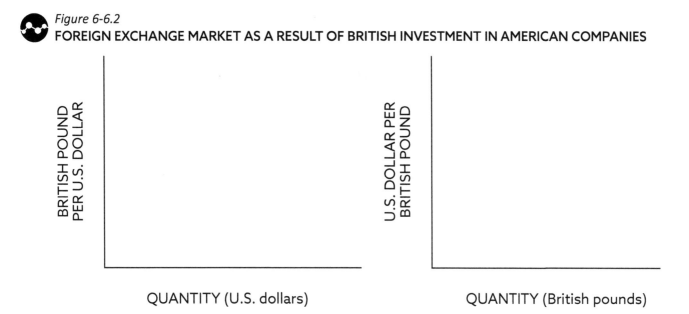

4.  The changes above will cause U.S. net exports to (increase/decrease).

5.  A US firm sells $5 million in tools and equipment to a firm in Mexico, where the currency is the peso. How will this transaction affect Mexico's Aggregate Demand? Using a correctly labeled graph of the foreign exchange rate for the US Dollar, show the value of the US Dollar relative to the Mexican peso.

*Figure 6-6.3*
**FOREIGN EXCHANGE MARKET AS A RESULT OF MEXICAN PURCHASE OF US GOODS**

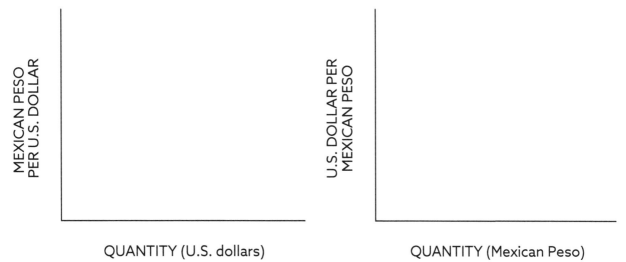

Answer:

6.  The value of the dollar against the peso (increases/decreases).

# Net Exports and Capital Flows: Linking Financial and Goods Markets

The loanable funds market is used to analyze capital flows in an economy. Because financial capital affects the amount of money available for borrowers, changes in capital flows shift the supply curve for loanable funds. Capital inflows increase the supply of loanable funds, resulting in the decrease in domestic real interest rates shown in Figure 6-7.1:

*Figure 6-7.1*
**CAPITAL INFLOWS INCREASE THE SUPPLY OF LOANABLE FUNDS**

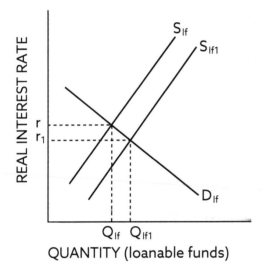

Capital outflows deplete a nation's supply of loanable funds, causing domestic interest rates to increase, as shown in the following graph:

*Figure 6-7.2*
**CAPITAL OUTFLOWS DEPLETE THE SUPPLY OF LOANABLE FUNDS**

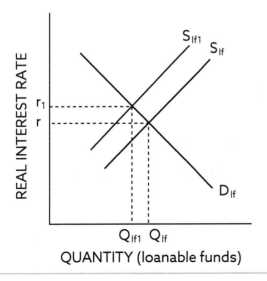

1. Illustrate on a correctly labeled graph of the loanable funds market in the United States the changes that result from the Japanese importation of U.S. semiconductors. *Hint:* Current account deficits are offset by capital and financial account surpluses (capital inflow) while current account surpluses are offset by capital and financial account deficits (capital outflow).

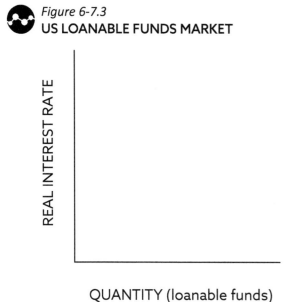

*Figure 6-7.3*
**US LOANABLE FUNDS MARKET**

REAL INTEREST RATE

QUANTITY (loanable funds)

2. Assume that inflation in the United States begins to rise while prices throughout the European Union remain relatively stable. The U.S. current account moves toward (surplus/deficit) and U.S. net exports (increase/decrease).

3. Illustrate on the graphs provided how the relative exchange rates of the U.S. dollar and euro will change as a result of this change in relative inflation rates. Be sure to label your graphs correctly (e.g., the price of dollars should be stated in terms of euro per dollar, and vice versa).

*Figure 6-7.4*
**RELATIVE EXCHANGE RATES OF THE US DOLLAR AND EURO**

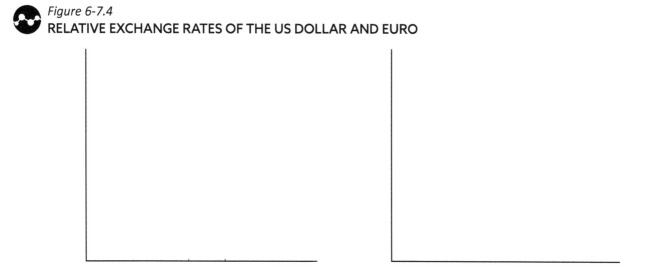

4.  Illustrate on a graph of the loanable funds market in the United States (Figure 6-7.5), the changes that result when the relative inflation rates change. *Hint:* Current account deficits are offset by capital and financial account surpluses (capital inflow) while current account surpluses are offset by capital and financial account deficits (capital outflow).

*Figure 6-7.5*
**US LOANABLE FUNDS MARKET**

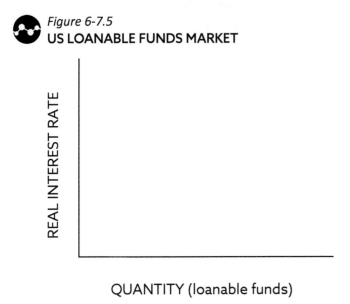

5.  Due to a recent recession, expansionary fiscal policies in the United States have led to historically large federal budget deficits. On a correctly labeled graph of the loanable funds market in the United States (Figure 6-7.6), illustrate the effects of massive government borrowing.

Rationale:

*Figure 6-7.6*
**US LOANABLE FUNDS MARKET**

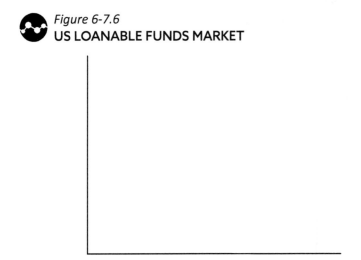

6.  The increased borrowing causes real interest rates to (increase/decrease) and foreign investors will (increase/decrease) their purchases of bonds in the United States. Illustrate this change on your loanable funds graph (Figure 6-7.6) above.

Rationale:

7.  Assume that the U.S. central bank enacts an expansionary policy of purchasing government securities on the open market. This monetary policy will (increase/decrease) real interest rates in the United States. As a result of the change in real interest rates, foreign investors will (increase/decrease) their purchases of bonds in the United States.

8.  Illustrate the effects of foreign investors changing their purchases of bonds on a correctly labeled graph of the loanable funds market in Figure 6-7.7.

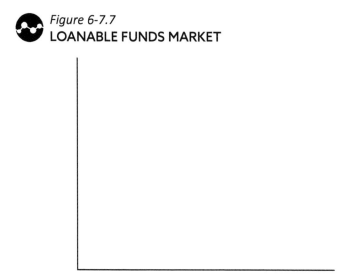

*Figure 6-7.7*
**LOANABLE FUNDS MARKET**

9.  Foreign direct investment (FDI) into the United States rose sharply during the second half of the 1990s due to the perceived strength and stability of the U.S. economy relative to unstable economies worldwide. On a correctly labeled graph of the loanable funds market in the United States, illustrate the effect of this influx of FDI.

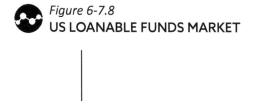

*Figure 6-7.8*
**US LOANABLE FUNDS MARKET**

REAL INTEREST RATE

QUANTITY (loanable funds)

10. The U.S. economy slowed in the early 2000s while American firms discovered less costly production possibilities in foreign countries. On a correctly labeled graph of the loanable funds market in the United States, illustrate the effects of this capital flight in Figure 6-7.9.

*Figure 6-7.9*
**US LOANABLE FUNDS MARKET**

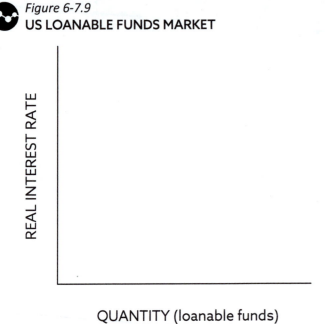